IN MEMORIAM

Das große Buch
der Trauerfloristik

Contemporary Funeral Design the ultimate collection

Mit Unterstützung von / Sponsored by

HALBACH
SEIDENBÄNDER

Bibliografische Information der Deutschen Bibliothek
Die Deutsche Bibliothek verzeichnet diese Publikation in der
Deutschen Nationalbibliografie; detaillierte bibliografische Daten
sind im Internet über http://dnb.ddb.de abrufbar.

Herausgeber / Publisher
FMS Floristik Marketing Service GmbH, Ratingen

Idee + Konzeption / Idea + Concept
Hella Henckel

Floristische Leitung / Floristic Direction
Klaus Wagener

Floristik / Floristry
Jan-Dirk von Hollen
Team 'profil floral'

Text + Redaktion / Text + Editor
Hella Henckel (vwtl. / Editor-in-Chief)
Sabine Nowak

Übersetzung / Translation
Janet Brümmer, Düsseldorf

Beratung / Consultant
J. W. Fretz, Vineland

Art Direktion / Art Direction
Carola John
Annika Kohnen

Bildredaktion / Photo Editing
Renate Haller

DTP / DTP
Kabir Kapoor
Michaela Gageik

Fotos / Photos
FMS / Patrick Pantze-Werbefotografie GmbH, Lage
FMS / g&v (1)

© 2004 Floristik Marketing Service GmbH (FMS)
Am Potekamp 6 – D-40885 Ratingen / Deutschland
Tel: +49-2102-9644-0, Fax: +49-2102-896073
E-mail: info@fms-online.de
1. Auflage 2004

ISBN 3-9809010-5-X

IMPRESSUM PRODUCTION TEAM

Consolation with flowers

When people need funeral flowers, the competent and understanding advice of florists or cemetery flower shops will have a considerable influence on the choice of design. This applies not only to the question of whether a wreath is enough or if more flowers are necessary for certain bereavement situations. As well, both parties must work together to find the right type of design with the individual customising needed to meet the specific requirements of the bereaved family.

People having to pick out funeral flowers are usually in an emotionally overloaded state. All too quickly, bereaved customers often go for the "standard" design without bothering to inquire about the wide range of possibilities for creating more personalised arrangements. Some may not realise that taking the time to make the right choice of funeral flowers will not only express more esteem and respectful remembrance of the deceased, but also help surviving family members to better overcome their grief.

This book is intended to assist in the creation, consulting and selection of funeral arrangements. For one, it is a user-friendly source of inspiration for helping the bereaved customer make difficult decisions at a difficult time, and for another it is a collection of design ideas that show those having to deal with grief and death on a professional level the huge scope of possibilities for making appealing and consoling funeral arrangements. In a competent and sensitive discussion on all that flowers can achieve for the mourning, a respectful and dignified solution is found that has a very consoling and comforting effect.

All of the arrangements shown in the book are meant to give you inspiration for your work. Of course you are free to choose different flowers or foliage, alter the size of the arrangement, or add some ribbon or mourning accessories to add your own personal touch. There's no right or wrong here, just some new ideas to implement with your own.

Florists and cemetery flower shops are well advised to offer their customers this book as a visual consulting aid. For the bereaved customer it offers a number of new impulses and ideas for achieving very personal funeral tributes, as well as a new insight into contemporary funeral design.

The service section on how to integrate ribbons in bouquets, wreaths or based tributes, as well the tips on how various foliage wreaths can be created, will provide helpful hints for everyone on how to customise and supplement the designs. No two assemblies are quite the same, and the result will often be a unique and personalised piece of floristic excellence.

The information on the symbolic significance of colours, flowers and shapes also offers new and helpful ideas and creative concepts.

Because mourning and sympathy often leave people feeling at a loss for words, this book also includes a selection of appropriate texts for sympathy cards or wreath banners. And last but not least: lists of all the materials used in the assemblies as well as useful information on technique for promoting the work of the florist or cemetery flower shop.

Today's funeral design stands for the preservation of tradition and honour on the one hand and contemporary floral interpretation and individuality on the other. The aim of this book is to provide helpful tips and inspiration for achieving this.

Mit Blumen trösten

Im Bereich der Trauerfloristik entscheidet eine gute, einfühlsame Beratung durch den Floristen oder Friedhofsgärtner maßgeblich über die blumige Ausgestaltung im Trauerfall. Dies bezieht sich nicht nur auf die Frage, ob es über den Kranz hinaus noch weitere Blumen für die Trauerfeier geben soll. Auch bei der Art der Ausführung und der individuellen Abstimmung auf den Verstorbenen ist die intensive Beschäftigung mit dieser Thematik der beiden beteiligten Seiten Voraussetzung.

Wer sich mit Trauerfloristik beschäftigen muss, ist meist in einer emotional angespannten Situation. Zu schnell greift da der Trauernde zum „Standard", ohne sich der Fülle und Möglichkeiten individueller Gestaltungen bewusst zu sein. Dabei liegen gerade in der richtigen und ruhigen Wahl der Trauerfloristik Wertschätzung und würdevolles Gedenken an den Verstorbenen sowie ein Stück Trauerbewältigung für den Hinterbliebenen.

Bei dieser Auswahl und bei der Beratung will dieses Buch Hilfestellung geben. Es soll den Trauerkunden bei seinem Entscheidungsprozess anschaulich unterstützen, aber auch denen von berufswegen mit Trauer und Tod Beschäftigten die Vielfalt trauerfloristischer Darstellungen aufzeigen. In der gekonnten und sensiblen Abstimmung und Übereinstimmung dessen, was Blumen leisten können, entsteht ein würdiger Rahmen, der tröstlich wirken kann.

Alle im Buch dargestellten Arrangements sind als Anregungen zu verstehen. Sie können durch die Wahl anderer Blumen oder Grünbestandteile, durch Veränderung der Größe, das Hinzufügen von Band oder trauerfloristischen Accessoires individuell abgewandelt werden. Nichts muss als gegeben hingenommen werden, sondern dient lediglich als Inspiration für die eigene Umsetzung.

Der Florist oder Friedhofsgärtner ist gut beraten, seinen Kunden dieses Buch als visuelle Beratungsunterlage vorzulegen. Dem Trauerkunden wird es eine Vielzahl neuer Impulse und Ansätze für seinen ganz persönlichen Trauerschmuck bieten und ihn zu einem neuen Verständnis von zeitgemäßer Trauerfloristik führen.

Die Serviceseiten zu Bandverarbeitung in Sträußen, an Kränzen oder Gestecken, sowie die Hinweise, wie unterschiedlich Blätterkränze gestaltet sein können, geben allen Beteiligten hilfreiche Hinweise für Abwandlungen, Veränderungen, Ergänzungen. Kein Werkstück gleicht dem anderen, immer wieder wird es sich um Unikate und persönliche Einzelanfertigungen handeln.

Die Hinweise auf die symbolische Bedeutung von Farben, Blumen oder Formen bieten darüber hinaus neue und weiterführende Denk- und Gestaltungsansätze.

Weil Trauer und Mitgefühl oft die Worte verstummen lassen, liefert dieses Buch außerdem eine Auswahl einfühlsamer Texte für Kondolenzschreiben oder für Kranzschleifen. Schließlich unterstützen die Listung aller verwendeten Werkstoffe sowie Technikangaben den Floristen oder Friedhofsgärtner bei seiner Arbeit.

Trauerfloristik von heute bedeutet Wahrung der Tradition und Ehrung einerseits und zeitgemäße Interpretation und Individualität andererseits. Dazu will das Buch Hilfestellung und viele Anregungen bieten.

VORWORT EDITORIAL

INHALT CONTENTS

KONDOLENZSTRÄUSSE SYMPATHY TRIBUTES

Anteilnahme mit
Sternblüten

Wie Blütensterne wirken die weißen Blüten der Lilien oder der Eucharis. Sie drücken Mitgefühl aus, ohne selbst zu traurig zu wirken.

Sympathy tribute
with star-shaped flowers

Like floral stars the white flowers of the lily or Eucharis express sympathy without appearing too sad themselves.

Gelb-weiße
Trauersträuße im Frühling

Augenweide und Trost in einem: Sträuße mit einer Vielzahl an Blüten und Zweigen im Gelb-Weiß-Bereich sind ein tröstlicher Anblick in einer traurigen Phase.

Yellow-and-white
tributes in spring

A sight for sore eyes and consolation in one: bouquets with a wide variety of flowers and twigs in the yellow-and-white spectrum are a comforting sight in a time of sorrow.

Handsträuße für Grab und Trauerhaus

Ob man die Blumengebinde als Gruß für die Hinterbliebenen oder als blumige Begleiter während der Beerdigung wählt, in jedem Fall werden sie offen als Strauß in der Hand getragen. Deshalb sollten die Stiele fest mit Naturbast umwickelt sein. So weisen sie auch keine umweltbelastenden oder unverrottbaren Bestandteile auf. Im Trauerhaus können sie wiederum zusammen mit der Bastumwicklung ins Wasser gestellt werden.

Hand bouquets for cemetery and home

Either as a sympathy tribute for the bereaved or as a floral escort during the funeral, in any case these creations are meant to be carried open as hand bouquets. For this reason, the stems should be bound securely with natural bast to make a handle. This way the entire piece is environmentally friendly, as every part of it will decay naturally. In the home of the bereaved the bouquets can be placed in water without removing the bast.

Sträuße mit besonderen Formen

Eine Blattmanschette, eine Trichterform aus Korkenzieherhasel oder ein Strauß in Kegelform ziehen aufgrund der Besonderheiten die Aufmerksamkeit auf sich. Die Beschäftigung mit Blumigem kann in einer Zeit der Trauer für Hinterbliebene ein Moment der tröstlichen Begleitung sein.

Bouquets with special shapes

A foliage edge, a funnel-shaped construction of corkscrew hazel or a bouquet in the shape of a cone will be guaranteed their share of the attention. Working with flowers can also be a comforting pastime for the bereaved during the mourning period.

Sträuße mit
Trauerakzenten

Ganz gleich, ob es ein eingebundener Trauerflor, eine kranzartige
Umwindung mit Jasmin und Kordeln oder die schneckenförmigen
Naturakzente sind: Solche Details sagen mehr als viele Worte.
Zusammen mit den Blumen drücken sie aus, was gesprochen oft so
schwer fällt, nämlich einfach Mitgefühl.

Bouquets with
mourning accents

Regardless of whether you integrate a mourning crepe, a wreath-like
encirclement of jasmine and cords or a snail-shaped accent of
natural materials, such details say more than many a spoken word.
Together with the flowers they help express sentiments that are
otherwise so difficult to utter: condolences.

Nelken im Stil der Siebziger

Nelken waren in den Siebzigern en vogue und sind jetzt wieder stark im Kommen. Für viele Menschen sind diese Blumen voller positiver Erinnerungen an Kindheit, Jugend oder unbeschwerte Erwachsenenzeit.

Carnations in seventies look

In the 1970s carnations were very much en vogue and are now enjoying resurgent popularity. For many people these flowers bring back fond memories of carefree times in childhood, youth or adult years.

Monoblumige Sträuße

Sowohl die Calla als auch die zuvor gezeigten Nelken brauchen nur
wenige Begleiter, weil sie von sich aus ausdrucksstark und dekorativ wirken.

Mono bouquets

Calla lilies and the carnations shown on the previous pages need
very few accompanying materials as they are very expressive and
decorative on their own.

Sträuße mit tröstlichen Blüten

Blüten wie das Tränende Herz, weiße Nelken oder die edle Lilie gelten seit jeher als Blumen mit Trauersymbolik. Sie in einen Trauerstrauß einzubinden, ist ein gefühlvolles Zeichen der Anteilnahme und des Gedenkens.

Bouquets with consoling flowers

Flowers like the bleeding heart, white carnations or the noble lily have always been regarded as having mourning symbolism. Integrating them into funeral arrangements is a sensitive gesture of sympathy and remembrance.

Sag es mit Blumen

Grün ist die Farbe der Hoffnung, Weiß die der Reinheit und Verklärung. Wo früher eine prächtige Blütenlast die innere Anteilnahme zum Ausdruck brachte, lässt die zeitgemäße Sprache mehr die Ästhetik der Einfachheit zu.

Say it with flowers

Green is the colour of hope, while white stands for purity and clarity. Where in the past more opulent bouquets were popular for expressing deep condolences, today sympathy is communicated through the contemporary aesthetics of simplicity.

Anteilnahme
mit weißen Blüten

Blüten in der Farbe der Reinheit. Weiß steht auch für Trauer und Kontemplation und drückt daher Anteilnahme aus. Besonders würdig ist es, weiße Blüten mit einem Trauerflor zu versehen.

Condolences
with white flowers

Flowers in the colour of purity, which also stands for mourning and contemplation, are always suitable for bereavements. It's a special sign of respect to add a mourning crepe to arrangements in white.

Wasserfall-Sträuße

Sie können auf einem hohen Gefäß ruhen und sich verneigend nach unten orientieren. Kaskadensträuße haben eine einseitig asymmetrische Form. Das macht sie passend für den Anlass. Als Überarmstrauß lassen sie sich sogar bei der Trauerfeier mitführen, um sie dann auf dem Grab oder dem Sarg abzulegen.

Cascade bouquets

These sympathy tributes can sit atop a tall container and drape elegantly down. Cascade bouquets have a one-sided asymmetrical form, which makes them very suitable for such occasions. As an arm sheath they can even be carried at the funeral service, and then placed on the grave or casket.

Violett, die Zuversicht

Violett ist eine christliche Farbe, die Besinnung und Glauben assozi-
iert. Wer diesen Ausdruck geben möchte, kann Sträuße in entsprechend farbigen Blüten wählen. Bänder unterstreichen zusätzlich die
christliche Zuversicht.

Violet, colour of faith

Violet is a religious colour associated with contemplation and faith.
Anyone desiring this expression can choose bouquets of flowers in
corresponding shades. Ribbons additionally underscore the symbol
of Christianity.

Handsträußchen in Weiß

Blumen trösten. Diese Aussage verwirklicht sich vor allem beim letzten Weg zur Ruhestätte. Hierbei einen Strauß in der Hand zu halten, um ihn mit dem Sarg zusammen ins Grab zu geben, ist vielen Menschen ein Bedürfnis.

Hand bouquet in white

Flowers are very consoling. This is especially true on the last journey to the final resting place. These bouquets are meant to be carried by hand to the grave to lay on the casket, something many people feel the need to do.

Sträußchen für den Gang zum Grab

Zum kleinen Bündel gefasste Sträußchen sind die passenden Begleiter für den Trauerzug. Sie lassen sich leicht in der Hand halten. Vor allem Frauen geben lieber als letzten Gruß Blumen oder Sträußchen anstelle einer Handvoll Erde mit ins Grab.

Posies for the funeral procession

A small bunch of flowers tied in a posy is perfect for a funeral procession. They are light and easy to carry. In particular, women prefer to use them as a last farewell at the grave in lieu of a handful of earth.

Einzelblüten zum Abschied

Rosen sind die passenden Blüten, um während der Trauerfeier und des Zuges zum Grab in der Hand getragen zu werden. Ein Brauch, der stark verbreitet ist und eine zarte Geste des Abschiednehmens darstellt.

Single blooms
for a final farewell

Roses are very suitable flowers for holding during the funeral service and for carrying to the grave. A custom that is widely propagated and that represents a tender gesture of farewell.

Manschetten-Sträußchen

Sind kleine Handsträußchen mit Manschetten umgeben, wertet dies die blumigen Gaben auf. Für enge Familienangehörige eine gute Möglichkeit, dadurch eine Differenzierung zu den Nachwerf-sträußchen für die übrigen Trauergäste vorzunehmen.

Collared bouquets

Adding a decorative collar to hand bouquets gives added value to the flowers. This is a good way to differentiate the floral grave tributes of close family members from those of the other mourners.

Die Trauerkarte am Trauerstrauß

Stilvolles, würdevolles Gedenken und Beileid werden meist zusätzlich durch eine Trauerkarte am Strauß ausgedrückt. Vorformulierte, einfühlsame Worte helfen dort, wo die eigenen verstummen. Dabei leisten zeitgemäße Trauerkarten mit den Worten von Literaten oder Dichtern, Zitate von Philosophen, Denkern oder aus der Bibel hilfreiche Unterstützung; einige dieser Trauersprüche sind auf der folgenden Seite aufgeführt. Die Trauerkarte sollte mit dem Strauß zusammen immer eine Einheit bilden. Statt Klebestreifen gibt es interessante Kreativlösungen, die die Karte nicht als Fremdkörper am Blumenschmuck erscheinen lassen.

Sympathy cards in funeral tributes

Tasteful, respectful remembrance and condolences are usually expressed additionally with a sympathy card. Carefully formulated, understanding words and phrases are very helpful when one is feeling at a loss for words. Contemporary cards with phrases borrowed from writers or poets, quotes from philosophers, great thinkers or from the Bible offer helpful support; some of these phrases are listed on the next page. Sympathy cards should always form a unit with the bouquet. Rather than using cello tape, there are lots of interesting, creative ways of attaching the card without it looking out of place in the arrangement.

Möglichkeit 1:
Die Trauerkarte kann mit Hilfe eines Grasbüschels und einer Drahtschlaufe befestigt werden. Das verbindet die schriftliche Botschaft mit der blumigen ohne gestalterische Einbußen.

Possibility 1:
The sympathy card can be attached with the help of a tuft of grass and a wire loop. This connects the written message and the floral one without affecting the design of the arrangement.

Möglichkeit 2:
Trauerkarte in einen gespleißten Zweig stecken, oben und unterhalb der Karte mit Bast abwickeln und einen Trauerflor anbringen.

Possibility 2:
Insert the sympathy card between the two halves of a split branch, bind the branch together with bast above and below the card and add a mourning ribbon.

Alles Wachsen ist ein Sterben,
jedes Werden ein Vergehen.
Alles Lassen ein Erleben,
jeder Tod ein Auferstehen. (R. Tagore)

What we call the beginning is often the end.
And to make an end is to make a beginning.
The end is where we start from. (T. S. Eliot)

Am Grunde des Herzens eines jeden
Winters liegt ein Frühlingsahnen.
(Khalil Gibran)

When the spring sings its hymn the dead of
the winter rise, shed their shrouds and
march forward. (Khalil Gibran)

Da ist ein Land der Lebenden und ein
Land der Toten. Und die Brücke zwischen
ihnen ist die Liebe – das einzig Bleibende,
der einzige Sinn. (Thornton Wilder)

There is a land of the living and a land of the
dead and the bridge is love, the only survival,
the only meaning. (Thornton Wilder)

Das einzig Wichtige im Leben sind die
Spuren von Liebe, die wir hinterlassen,
wenn wir weggehen. (Albert Schweitzer)

The only important thing in life: the traces
of love we leave behind. (Albert Schweitzer)

Und ein Flügelpaar faltet sich los! Dorthin!
Ich muss! Ich muss! Gönnt mir den Flug!
(J. W. von Goethe)

In the night of death, hope sees a star,
and listening love can hear the rustle
of a wing. (Robert Ingersoll)

Gefühlvolle Worte für traurige Momente

Compassionate thoughts for solom moments

Denn er hat seinen Engeln befohlen, dass sie dich behüten auf allen deinen Wegen, dass sie dich auf den Händen tragen und du deinen Fuß nicht an einen Stein stoßest. (Psalm 91, 11-12)

For He shall give his angels charge over thee, to keep thee in all thy ways. They shall bear thee up in their hands, lest thou dash thy foot against a stone. (Psalm 91, 11-12)

Die Erinnerung ist das einzige Paradies, aus dem wir nicht vertrieben werden können. (Jean Paul)

Recollection is the only paradise from which we cannot be turned out. (Jean Paul)

Eines Morgens wachst du nicht mehr auf, die Vögel aber singen wie sie gestern sangen. Nichts ändert diesen neuen Tagesablauf. Nur du bist fortgegangen – Du bist nun frei und unsere Tränen wünschen dir Glück. (J. W. von Goethe)

Because I could not stop for Death, He kindly stopped for me. The Carriage held but just ourselves and Immortality. (Emily Dickinson)

Für jetzt bleiben Glaube, Hoffnung, Liebe, diese drei; doch am größten unter ihnen ist die Liebe. (Die Bibel, 1. Korinther 13,13)

And now these three remain: faith, hope and love. But the greatest of these is love. (The Bible, 1 Corinthians 13,13)

Ich glaube, dass wenn der Tod unsere Augen schließt, wir in einem Lichte stehen, von welchem unser Sonnenlicht nur der Schatten ist. (Arthur Schopenhauer)

I believe that when death closes our eyes we shall awaken to a light, of which our sunlight is but the shadow. (Arthur Schopenhauer)

Mit den Flügeln der Zeit fliegt die Traurigkeit davon. (Jean de La Fontaine)

Sadness flies away on the wings of time. (Jean de La Fontaine)

Tod hat keine Bedeutung. Ich bin nur einen Raum weiter gegangen. Ich bleibe wer ich bin. Und auch ihr bleibt dieselben. Was wir einander bedeuten, bleibt bestehen. Nennt mich mit einem vertrauten Namen, sprecht in der gewohnten Weise mit mir und ändert dabei euren Tonfall nicht. Hüllt euch nicht in Mäntel aus Schweigen und Kummer. Lacht wie immer über die kleinen Scherze, die wir teilten. Wenn ihr von mir sprecht, so tut es ohne Reue und ohne jegliche Traurigkeit. Leben bedeutet immer Leben. Es bleibt bestehen – immer, ohne Unterbrechung. Ihr seht mich nicht, aber in Gedanken bin ich bei euch. Ich warte eine Zeitlang auf euch. Irgendwo, ganz in der Nähe. Alles ist gut. (Henry Scott Holland)

Death is nothing at all. I have only slipped away into the next room. I am I, you are you. Whatever we were to each other, that we still are. Call me by my old familiar name, speak to me in the easy way you always used to. Put no difference in your tone, wear no forced air of solemnity or sorrow. Laugh as we always laughed at the little jokes we enjoyed together. Let my name be ever the household word it always was, let it be spoken without effort, without the trace of a shadow on it. Life means all that it ever meant. Why should I be out of mind because I am out of sight? I am waiting for you, for an interval, somewhere very near, just round the corner. All is well. (Henry Scott Holland)

Tod muss so schön sein. In der weichen, braunen Erde liegen, während über unserem Kopf das Gras wogt. Und der Stille lauschen, kein gestern haben und kein morgen. Die Zeit vergessen, dem Leben verzeihen – in Frieden sein. (Oscar Wilde)

Death must be so beautiful. To lie in the soft brown earth, with the grasses waving above one's head, and listen to silence. To have no yesterday, and no tomorrow. To forget time, to forgive life, to be at peace. (Oscar Wilde)

Und wenn Du dich getröstet hast, wirst Du froh sein, mich gekannt zu haben. Du wirst immer mein Freund sein. Du wirst dich daran erinnern, wie gerne Du mit mir gelacht hast. (Antoine de Saint-Exupéry)

He who has gone, so we but cherish his memory, abides with us, more potent, nay, more present than the living man. (Antoine de Saint-Exupéry)

Von guten Mächten wunderbar geborgen Erwarten wir getrost, was kommen mag. Gott ist mit uns am Abend und am Morgen Und ganz gewiss an jedem neuen Tag. (Dietrich Bonhoeffer)

For what is it to die, but to stand in the sun and melt into the wind? (Kahlil Gibran)

Wir kommen weit her liebes Kind und müssen weit gehen. Keine Angst. Alle sind bei Dir. Die vor Dir waren. Deine Mutter, Dein Vater und alle, die vor ihnen waren. Weit, weit zurück. Alle sind bei Dir. Keine Angst. Wir kommen weit her und müssen weit gehen, liebes Kind. (Heinrich Böll)

Deep hearts, wise minds, take life as God has made it. It is a long trial; An unintelligible preparation for an unknown destiny. This destiny, the true one, begins for man at the first step in the interior of the tomb. There he begins to discern the definite. The definite, think of this word! The living see the infinite; the definite reveals itself only to the dead. Meantime, love and suffer, hope and contemplate. Woe, alas! to him who shall have loved forms, bodies, appearances only. Death will take all from him. Try to love souls, you shall find them again. (Victor Hugo)

Die Sprache der Blumen im Trauerstrauß

Was macht einen Strauß zu einem Trauer- oder Kondolenzstrauß? Zum einen kann sich dieser aufgrund seiner Gestaltung als Ausdruck des Mitgefühls und des Gedenkens darstellen. Dabei kommt eine leicht überhängende, wasserfallartige Form, die an Tränen, an das Passive des Leidens und Trauerns erinnert, der Situation, für die der Strauß gewählt wird, entgegen. Zum anderen machen Accessoires, die den Anlass widerspiegeln, ein Blumengebinde zum Trauerstrauß. Hierzu zählen Trauerbänder – mit oder ohne aufgedruckte Worte – Trauerflor, die Kondolenzkarte oder kleine Symbole wie Herzen oder Kreuze. In jedem Fall ist es aber auch die Auswahl der Blumen, die Trauersträuße von sonstigen unterscheidet. Gefühlvolle und symbolträchtige Blumen wie Nelken und Calla bieten sich dabei an, aber auch viele andere Blumen geben Trauersträußen eine Aussage und Bedeutung.

The language of flowers in funeral tributes

What makes a bouquet a funeral or sympathy tribute? For one, its inherent design represents the expression of condolence and commemoration. The shape can also be significant, for example a teardrop or cascading bouquet stands for tears, the passive aspect of bereavement, the occasion for which the bouquet has been chosen. At the same time special accessories that reflect the occasion can transform a floral assembly into a funeral arrangement. For example, wreath banners – either with or without words printed on them – mourning ribbons, sympathy cards or small symbols such as hearts or crosses. But in any case, the choice of flowers is what mostly differentiates a funeral arrangement from other floral bouquets. Symbolic flowers that express deep emotions, such as carnations and Calla lilies, are ideal although there is a host of other flowers that can also give sympathy tributes special meaning.

Akazie
(Acacia)
Überwinde den Tod.
Acacia
May you be blessed with
eternal life.

Buchsbaum
(Buxus sempervirens)
Es kommt ein anderes Leben.
Sei stark!
Box
A new life is born. Be strong!

Dattelpalme
(Phoenix canariensis)
Besiege den Tod.
Friede sei mit dir.
Date palm
May you be blessed with eternal
life. Peace be with you.

Distel
(Carduus defloratus)
Christus hat den Tod überwunden,
du wirst ihn auch überwinden!
Thistle
The Lord himself goes before
you and will always be with you!

Efeu
(Hedera helix)
Unsere Treue und Freundschaft
begleite dich!
Ivy
There is comfort in friendship.

Ehrenpreis
(Veronica spicata)
Du wirst gerettet.
Speedwell
The Lord will save you.

Eibe
(Taxus baccata)
Sei beschützt vor bösen Mächten.
Deine Seele bleibe unsterblich.
Yew
May you be delivered from the
powers of evil. Your soul will
forever be with us.

Eiche
(Quercus robus)
Die Kraft verlasse dich nicht.
Oak
May you always be strong.

Färberkamille
(Anthemis tinctoria)
Sie schütze dich durch ihre Kräfte.
Yellow chamomile
This flower protects you with
its strength.

Kalla
(Zantedeschia aethiopica)
Besiege den Tod. Licht und
Klarheit umgeben dich.
Calla
May you be blessed with
eternal life. May light and clarity
surround you.

Lilie
(Lilium longiflorum)
Licht und Klarheit begleiten dich!
Lily
May light and clarity be with you!

Lorbeer
(Laurus nobilis)
Sei stark in Ewigkeit, ewige Kraft
und Jugendlichkeit begleiten dich!
Siege über den Tod.
Bay
May eternal strength and youth
always be with you! May you be
blessed with eternal life.

Maiglöckchen
(Convallaria majalis)
Das Paradies wartet auf dich!
Lily-of-the-valley
Paradise awaits you!

Narzisse
(Narcissus)
Überwinde den Tod!
Narcissus
May you be blessed with
eternal life!

Nelke
(Dianthus)
Überwinde den Tod!
Carnation
May you be blessed with
eternal life!

Olive
(Olea europaea)
Friede sei mit dir.
Olive
Peace be with you.

Ringelblume
(Calendula officinalis)
Sei erlöst!
Marigold
Redemption be yours!

Rose
(Rosa)
Die Schönheit des Lebens begleite
dich. Die Liebe bleibt. Kraft im
Leiden. Überwinde den Tod.
Rose
May the beauty of life go with you.
There is comfort in the strength of
love. Hope in the midst of sorrow.
May you be blessed with
eternal life.

Rosmarin
(Rosmarinus officinalis)
Es schütze dich vor dem Bösen.
Rosemary
May you be delivered from
the powers of evil.

Schafgarbe
(Achillea millefolium)
Wir weinen um dich.
Common yarrow
We cry for you.

Schlafmohn
(Papaver somniferum)
Ruhe in einem tiefen,
erquickenden Schlaf.
Opium poppy
Rest in a deep, peaceful sleep.

Schwertlilie
(Iris)
Reinheit begleite dich, die
Sünde sei fern von dir!
Iris
May purity be with you,
may your sins be absolved!

Stiefmütterchen
(Viola tricolor)
Glaube, Hoffnung, Liebe bleiben.
Pansy
Faith, hope and love remain.

Strohblume
(Helichrysum)
Deine Seele ist unsterblich!
Strawflower
Your soul will forever be with us!

Tausendschön
(Bellis perennis)
Unsere Tränen begleiten dich.
Daisy
Our tears go with you.

Tulpe
(Tulipa)
Das Irdische ist vergänglich,
dein Name bleibt ewiglich.
Tulip
Earthly existence is transitory,
your name will live forever.

Vergissmeinnicht
(Myosotis communis)
Wenn Du auch stirbst,
wir sind an Liebe reich.
Forget-me-not
Even if you are gone,
we are blessed with love.

URNENSCHMUCK URN DECORATION

Mit Blüten umkränzt

Hier besteht der Urnenschmuck aus umgelegten Blüten-
ketten und Blütenkränzchen oder aus den Rosenzweigen, die rechts
und links neben der Säule mit der Urne postiert sind.

Encircled with flowers

Here the urn decorations consist of floral chains and small wreaths
draped around the urn or the rose branches positioned on the right
and left of the pillar holding the urn.

Gepflanzter Blütenschmuck

Schmuck für die Trauerfeierlichkeit und für das anschließende Urnengrab kann ein bepflanzter Kranz oder eine Schale sein. Auf einer Säule finden diese ihren Platz während der Trauerfeier.

Planted decorations

Decorations for the funeral service and then later for the urn grave can consist of a planted wreath or a planted container. During the funeral service it finds its niche on top of the pillar.

Blütenbasis

Die Kugel oder der florale Mantel stimmen als symbolhafte Aussagen tröstlich. Sie sind tragende Elemente und Erhöhung der Urne zugleich.

Floral base

The spherical holder or the floral covering are a symbolic message that sets a comforting mood. They serve to support and elevate the urn at the same time.

Blütenkissen

Ein tröstlicher Anblick, wie die Urne inmitten des kissenartigen Sockels aus Blüten ruht. Ein florales Herz kann die Urne liebevoll umschließen oder schützend bergen.

Floral cushion

A comforting sight, with the urn resting in the centre of a soft pillow of flowers. A floral heart provides a loving nest for the small urn or encircles it protectively.

Urnengalerie

So unterschiedlich wie die Form und das Material für Urnen können die kleinen floralen Schmuckakzente sein. Hier von klassisch bis romantisch-verspielt.

Urn gallery

As diversified as the shapes and materials of the urns, so can the small floral decorations be too. Here we run the gamut from classic to playful romantic.

Umkränzungen

Nicht allein die Fülle oder Menge der Blumen gilt als Maßstab der Wertschätzung, die die Hinterbliebenen dem Verstorbenen entgegen bringen. Vielmehr ist es die gefühlvolle und gestalterisch-kreative Ausstrahlung der jeweiligen Schmuckform, die die Aussage bringt. Die Variation der unterschiedlichen Urnenumkränzungen zeigt die Vielfalt dessen, was im Bereich Urnenschmuck möglich ist.

Encirclements

The wealth and abundance of the flowers in the arrangement for a loved one are not the only criteria for its value in the eyes of the bereaved. More than that, it is the emotional and creative aura of a design that expresses the desired message. The variation of different urn wreaths shows the wide scope of possibilities for adorning a cremation urn.

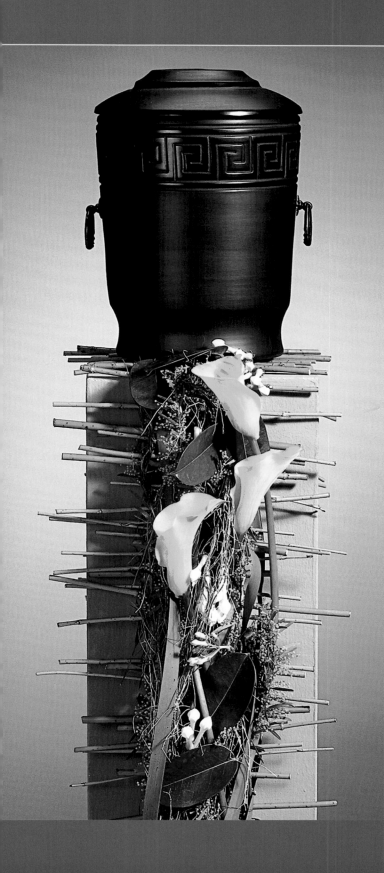

Säulengestaltung

Nicht immer muss die Urne selbst geschmückt werden. Auch die Präsentationsfläche, wie hier die Säule, bietet sich für eine Trost bringende Dekoration an.

Pillar design

No one says that the urn itself must always be decorated. Alternatively, the presentation area, for example the pillar here, makes a comforting eye-catcher.

Florale Akzentuierungen

Regelrechte Farbtupfer bilden die Blüten, klassisch muten die Kränzchen oder gereihten Blütenblätter an. Trockenfloralien ergeben einen lange haltbaren Schmuckakzent.

Floral accents

Some flowers are real colour highlights. Small wreaths or petals strung on wires have an almost timeless look. Dried materials provide a long-lasting decorative accent.

Rankenumspielungen

Ranken in jeglicher Form bieten sich aufgrund ihrer Zartheit an, um sie um Urnen zu winden oder zu legen. Das kann nahezu verhüllend sein, wie bei den beiden dunklen Urnen, oder als grüner Akzent zu einem Urnenschmuckband, wie bei der hellen Holzurne.

Vine encirclements

Thanks to their delicate tendrils, vines of every kind are very suitable for winding or placing around funeral urns. The effect can be either very closed, as in the case of the two dark-coloured urns here, or as a botanical accent for a decorative urn ribbon, for example the pale wooden one here.

Blütenreihung

Einfacher und dennoch mit der gebotenen Würde geht es kaum noch: Hier sind Laubblätter, Nadeln und Blütenblätter aufgefädelt und um die Urnen gelegt. Ein Ausdruck für die Fülle des Lebens.

Floral and foliage chains

Couldn't be much simpler – and yet the necessary respect is observed. Here a combination of leaves, needles and flower petals are strung on wires and arranged around the urns. An expression of the fullness of life.

Bandschmuck

Blütenblätter und Blättchen sind in das gehäkelte Band mit eingearbeitet und akzentuieren damit auf besondere Weise die ausgefallene und ohnehin auffällige Urne.

Decorative band

Flower petals and tiny leaves are integrated in the crocheted band to accentuate this unusual and eye-catching urn.

Bandschmuck an Urnen

Bei der Dekoration von Urnen wird noch viel zu wenig auf die schmückende Akzentuierung durch Bänder und Kordel zurück gegriffen. Dabei könnten auch hierfür die Bänder mit einem persönlichen Abschiedsgruß oder auch nur dem Namen der Hinterbliebenen bedruckt werden. Vor allem aber die Kombination von unterschiedlich farbigen Bändern oder solchen von unterschiedlicher Beschaffenheit schafft eine neue Dimension individueller Gestaltung. Kordeln, Litzen, Seiden- oder Taftbänder, solche mit und ohne Kantenbetonung – die Auswahl und die Farben lassen kaum Wünsche offen.

Ribbon decorations on urns

Urn embellishments still don't include enough decorative accentuation in the form of ribbons and cords, despite the obvious dual functionality of printing a personal farewell or the name of the bereaved on banners. Particularly the combination of various kinds of ribbons in all different colours and textures creates a new dimension in individual creativity. Cords, braids, silk and taffeta ribbons, either with or without fancy edging – the huge selection and wide range of colours leave hardly any wish unfulfilled.

SARGSCHMUCK CASKET DECORATION

Bogenschmuck
in Weiß-Grün

Der Sargbogen zieht sich asymmetrisch auf dem Sargdeckel ruhend quer über diesen und bildet damit einen ganz besonderen Schmuckakzent. So behält der Sarg seine Eigenwirkung.

Casket crescent
in green and white

This crescent-shaped spray is draped asymmetrically over the top of the casket, forming a very peaceful and decorative sympathy arrangement. And discreet enough to allow the casket its own show.

Blütenhaube
in klassisch Weiß

Weiß, die Farbe des Todes, der Trauer und der vollkommenen Reinheit, ist hier in eleganter, würdiger Form blumig gestaltet. Auch duftende Blumen, wie der Flieder und die Lilien, sind mit der Todessymbolik eng verbunden. Nach altem Volksglauben sollen sie dem Entschlafenen helfen, Dämonen abzuwehren.

Casket spray
in classic white

White, the colour of death, of bereavement and absolute purity, is florally interpreted in this elegant, dignified form. Even perfumed flowers, such as lilacs and lilies, are closely associated with the symbolism of death. According to popular beliefs they help the deceased to ward off demons.

Quer gelegte Blütenbögen

Der schlichte Sarg wird von einem üppigen, blütenreichen Bogen überspannt. Trotz der Fülle kommt die ansprechende Oberfläche des Holzsargs gut zur Wirkung. Kerzen können während der Trauerfeierlichkeit daneben noch Platz finden.

Vertically placed crescent spray

A relatively plain casket adorned with a stunning crescent bouquet placed vertically. Despite its opulence the tribute does not detract from the attractive finish of the wooden casket. A few candles could still find enough space beside it during the funeral service.

Gepflanzter Schmuck

Es müssen nicht immer Schnittblumen sein. Auch blühende Pflanzen und Gräser können einen Sarg schmücken, wenn der Untergrund entsprechend vorbereitet ist. Dies ergibt eine länger haltbare Pflanzengestaltung. Ihr Vorteil: Die Pflanzmatte kann bei der Bestattung abgenommen werden und als erste Grabbepflanzung dienen.

Planted tribute

There are other alternatives to cut flowers. Flowering plants and grasses can also decorate a casket if the surface is properly protected beforehand. The added benefit: a more lasting floral tribute that can be removed after the obsequies and used to adorn the fresh grave at the cemetery.

Blütenwolke

Wie eine duftige Wolke wirkt dieser Blütenschmuck, der von den tausend kleinen Blütchen des Schleierkrauts umgeben ist. Das lockert die farbenfrohe, flächige Blütengestaltung auf dem Sargdeckel zart und verspielt auf.

Floral cloud

This floral arrangement is as light and airy as a cloud, covered in masses of tiny blossoms of baby's breath. This loosens up the gaily-coloured, spreading tribute on the top of the casket in a tender and playful way.

Flach besteckter Blütendeckel

Die sommerliche, blütenreiche Bedeckung des schlichten Sarges bietet einen tröstlichen Anblick für die Hinterbliebenen. Mit der Mischfarbe Violett wird farbsymbolisch das irdische Rot mit dem himmlischen Blau versöhnt und verbunden.

Flat floral casket spray

The summery masses of flowers covering the top of the plain casket offer a comforting sight for the bereaved. With violet, a mix of blue and red the tribute symbolises the red earth and blue sky united in peace and harmony.

Gesteck in
warmen Sommerfarben

Von jeher sind Särge mit Floralem als Zeichen der Würdigung und Ehrerbietung geschmückt worden. Vielfach wurden und werden dafür Palmwedel verwendet, das Symbol für Leben und Auferstehung. Hier erfüllen Farnwedel diese Funktion. Sie geben dem blütenreichen Schmuck eine farbliche Ergänzung und Basis.

Casket spray
in warm summer hues

Caskets have always been decorated with florals as a sign of deference and respect. A popular material for this is always palm fronds, the symbol of life and resurrection. Here the green fronds play this role, as they provide a wonderful match and a secure basis for the colourful arrangement.

93

Pyramidales Blütengesteck

Die Opulenz des großen Sarggestecks lässt sich mit der Vielfalt des sommerlichen Blütenflors bestens erreichen. Ein Sargschmuck für einen Menschen, der einen starken Naturbezug hatte.

Pyramidal floral spray

The opulence of this eye-catching casket spray is best achieved with a wide diversity of summery flowers. The perfect casket decoration for someone who in life felt close to nature.

Rosenbouquets

Rosen stehen für die Ewigkeit und sind Ausdruck intensiver Gefühle.
Mit der spiraligen Kreisform symbolisieren sie Ewigkeit, mit dem dun-
kelroten Buchenlaub tiefe Trauer.

Rose bouquets

Roses stand for eternity and are the expression of intense feelings.
With the spiral shape they symbolise eternal life, and with the dark
beech leaves deep sorrow.

Rosengesteck in Dunkelrot

Ein prächtiges Sarggesteck, ganz in Dunkelrot gehalten. Das drückt Liebe und tiefe Zuneigung zu dem Verstorbenen aus. Deshalb eignet sich diese Art des Blütenschmucks ideal als letzter Gruß der nahen Angehörigen.

Rose tribute in dark-red

A magnificent casket spray, all in shades of rich red. The ultimate expression of love and deep devotion for the deceased. A sympathy tribute ideally suited for a last farewell from close relatives.

Rosenblüten-Dreieck

Ein schlichter Blütenschmuck aus Rosen in verschiedenen Gelb-, Creme- bis Champagnertönen. Das Besondere ist die dreieckige Anordnung auf dem flachen Sargdeckel und die Randakzentuierung in Form leicht gebogener Blätter.

Rose petal triangle

A simple floral tribute composed of roses in various shades of yellow, cream and champagne. The special feature is the three-cornered arrangement on the flat top of the casket with its foliage edge of gently curving leaves.

Kranz als Ewigkeitssymbol

Das Kranz- oder Ringsymbol auf dem Sarg weist auf das Immer-
wiederkehrende des Lebens hin. Der Lichtkranz drumherum greift
diese Symbolik auf.

The wreath
as symbol of eternity

The wreath or ring symbol on the casket is a reference to the circle
of life. The ring of candles around the outside reflects the
symbolism again.

Kranzauflage

Besonders einfachen Sargformen kann mit einem klassisch-schlich-
ten Kranzschmuck entsprochen werden. Einmal ein Blätterkranz auf
langer Blütenranke, das andere Mal ein Blütenband auf goldenem
Kranzsymbol.

Wreath tribute

Particularly simple casket designs can easily be adorned with a classic and simple wreath. Whether a leafy wreath on a long flowering
vine, or a chain of flowers on a golden symbol of eternity.

Girlandenschmuck

Ob in Wellenform oder straff um den Sarg gelegt: Der klassizistisch anmutende Girlandenschmuck wirkt vor allem durch seine gleichmäßige, akkurate Gestaltung. Dabei können die verschiedenfarbigen Blüten gereiht oder gleichmäßig gestreut über die Girlande verteilt werden, ganz nach Belieben. Weiße und gelbe Blumen gelten als Symbole der Reinheit und Hoffnung.

Garland decoration

Whether in a wavy pattern or as a straight line around the edge of the casket, the classic garland decoration is an eye-catcher with its even, accurate design. The flowers in different colours can either be arranged in monochrome rows or scattered around the entire garland, as you like. White and yellow flowers are considered symbols of purity and hope.

Rankenschmuck

An schlichte Särge schmiegt sich Rankenschmuck harmonisch an, so auch die bogenförmig sich verneigende Calla. Die sieben Stufen zur Glückseligkeit scheinen dagegen die flattrigen Ranken des Zierspargels zu erklimmen.

Vine decoration

Viny decorations cling harmoniously to plain caskets, for example this crescent-shaped sheath of Calla lilies. In contrast, the trembling tendrils of decorative asparagus appear to ascend the seven steps to spiritual happiness.

Sargkreuze

Je schlichter der Sarg, desto aussagekräftiger und dominanter darf der Schmuck sein. Knorrige Zweige bilden die christliche Symbolform des Kreuzes. Im reizvollen Kontrast dazu farbintensive Blüten und Früchte oder Rosen.

Casket crosses

The simpler the casket, the more expressive and dominant the tribute may be. Gnarled branches form the Christian symbol of the cross. In charming contrast are the brightly coloured flowers and fruit or roses.

KRÄNZE WREATHS

Vergänglichkeit
und Erneuerung

Frische Blumen auf wintertrockenem Laub. Das Leben ist vergäng-
lich, es sucht sich aber auch immer wieder neue Formen des Seins.
Erblühen und Vergehen liegen so nah beieinander wie Frühling und
Winter.

Transience
and rejuvenation

Fresh flowers on a winter dry wreath of leaves. Life is transient, but
we are always searching for new forms of existence. Blossoming
and dying are as closely associated as spring and winter.

Spuren des Lebens

Ein mit Frühlingsblühern bepflanzter Kranz ist nicht nur ein farben-
prächtiger Anblick. Die ersten Knospen und Blüten nach dem Winter
symbolisieren auch hoffnungsfroh ein neues Leben. Vergissmeinnicht stehen wider das Vergessen.

Traces of life

A wreath that is planted with spring flowers is not only a beautiful
array of lovely colours. The first buds and blossoms after the winter
ends also symbolise hopes for a new life. Forget-me-nots stand for
remembering.

Linien des Lebens

Die ausgewogene Verteilung der Strukturen und Farben stehen in diesen Linienkränzen als Stellvertreter für die Harmonie im Lebenslauf.

Lifelines

The balanced distribution of the different structures and colours in these starburst wreaths are representatives of harmony along life's path.

Vielfalt des Lebens

Kranzdekorationen aus dem Frühlings- und Sommerflor,
aus Heimischem und Fremdem, aus Blüten und
Früchten spiegeln die Vielfalt der Vegetation
wider und symbolisieren die Vielgestaltigkeit
des Lebens.

Variety of life

Wreath decorations featuring
spring and summer flora, both
domestic and imported,
from flowers to fruit,
reflect the diversity of
vegetation and sym-
bolise the many
facets of human
life.

Erneuerung

Holz steht für Kraft, seine Rinde für das sich stetig erneuernde Leben.
Diese rauen, aber sehr natürlich anmutenden Kränze haben in Kombination mit frischen Blätterzweigen eine tröstende Aussage.

Rejuvenation

Wood stands for strength, its bark for the constant rejuvenation of
life. These coarse yet very natural-looking wreaths, in combination
with fresh foliage, send a very consoling message.

Weiß,
die Farbe des Lichtes

Weiß, die Farbe der Reinheit und des Lichtes, verbindet sich gut mit Grün, der Farbe der Hoffnung. Doch auch dunkelgrüne und leicht gräuliche Changierungen geben diesen Kränzen eine besondere, würdige Ausstrahlung.

White,
the colour of light

White, the colour of purity and light, combines well with green, the colour of hope. But dark-green and green with a touch of grey also give these wreaths a special, dignified aura.

Grün ist die Hoffnung

Die Farbe wandelt sich zur Hoffnungssymbolik. Grün steht für Kraft und Leben und für die Zuversicht auf ein Leben nach dem Tod. Diese schlichten, ruhig wirkenden Kränze können zudem mit einem Kranzschleifenschmuck versehen werden.

Green means hope

The colour green becomes a symbol of hope. Green stands for strength and life and for the belief in life after death. These simple, peaceful-looking wreaths can also be decorated with ribbons or banners.

Blüten voller Würde

Weiße Blüten pur sind ein tröstlicher und würdiger Anblick. Ob Lilie oder die tausend Schleierkrautblüten – Variationen hierzu bietet die Blütenvielfalt des Sommers reichlich.

Flowers full of dignity

White flowers on their own are a consoling and dignified sight. Whether lilies or baby's breath by the thousands– variations on this theme are offered by the huge diversity of summer flora.

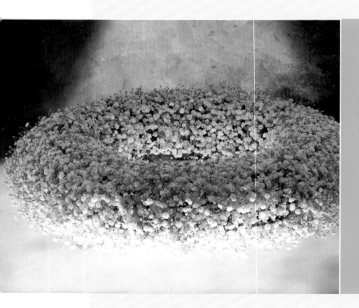

Kranz im Farbkreis

So vielfältig wie das Leben selbst ist dieser Kranz in den Farben des Regenbogens. Die Farbflächen stehen für die vier Jahreszeiten und symbolisieren zugleich die Abschnitte eines menschlichen Lebenslaufs.

Wreath in colour circle

As diversified as life itself is this wreath in the colours of the rainbow. The sections of colour stand for the four seasons and symbolise at the same time the phases of a human life story.

Blau wie die Treue

Die Erinnerung ist ein ewiges Band, das uns mit einem geliebten Menschen verbindet. Die Kränze in Blau sind farbintensive Überbringer der Botschaft: „Ich werde dich nie vergessen".

True blue

Memories are an never-ending circle, connecting us to a loved one. The wreaths in blue are brightly-coloured bearers of the message: "I'll never forget you".

Kränze mit blauem Band

Ob Blüten- oder Laubkränze: Band schmückt das tröstliche Rund in jedem Fall. Zusätzlich kann dieses noch für eine persönliche, verbale Botschaft genutzt werden – je nach Art und Breite des Bandes.

Wreaths with blue ribbons

Whether flowers or foliage wreaths: in any case ribbon decorates the consoling circle. Additionally, the sash can be used for a personal, verbal message – depending on the width of the banner.

Farben des Himmels

So wie der Himmel in allen Nuancen von Hellblau bis Tiefviolett leuchtet, ist dieser Kranz aus einer Fülle sommerlich-blauer Blüten gestaltet.

Shades of heaven

Reminiscent of skies awash with every nuance from palest blue to deep purple, this wreath is based with an abundance of summer flowers.

Romantische Trostspender

Wicken als Inbegriff sommerlicher Leichtigkeit und Unbeschwertheit: duftende Begleiter in Zeiten der Trauer.

Romantic sympathy tribute

Sweet peas are the quintessence of summertime lightness and carefree feelings: sweet-scented escorts in times of mourning.

Millefleurs-Kranz in Weiß

Hier wird die Reinheit und Klarheit durch weiße Blütenvielfalt besonders zart und verträumt ausgedrückt. Ein Kranz, der tröstliche Zuversicht vermittelt.

Millefleurs wreath in white

Here the purity and clarity of the colour white are expressed particularly gently and dreamily by the white mixture of a thousand flowers. A wreath that communicates faith.

Millefleurs

Die Kränze der „tausend Blüten" sind tröstliche Blickpunkte für die Trauernden. Sie wirken leicht und ebenmäßig und strahlen liebevolle Weichheit aus.

Millefleurs

The wreaths of a "thousand flowers" are consoling eye-catchers for those in mourning. They look light and evenly-proportioned and exude an aura of gentle sweetness.

Dornröschen-Kranz

Kinderschlaflieder besingen bereits das schützende Bedecktsein mit Rosen und anderen Blüten. Eine schöne Metapher für den Tod als erquickender Schlaf für das, was danach kommt.

Sleeping beauty wreath

Brahms lullaby already sang about a bed being "with roses bedight" and other flowers "o'erspread". A lovely metaphor for death as a refreshing sleep for a life that is over or one that is yet to come.

Rosen-Allerlei

Die Vielfalt der Gestaltungsmöglichkeiten mit Rosen ist schier unerschöpflich. Vor allem im Sommer bietet sich eine bezaubernde Fülle der Schönsten aller Blüten.

Medley of roses

The scope of creativity when working with roses is almost inexhaustible. Particularly in summer the abundance of cultivars of the Queen of Flowers is captivating.

Rosen und mehr

Nicht nur solo, auch mit anderen Blüten, Gräsern, Fruchtständen oder Blättern lassen sich Rosenblüten kombinieren. Die Vielfalt ist unendlich und symbolisiert damit auch die Unendlichkeit und die Vielgestaltigkeit des Lebens.

Roses and more

Not only solo, roses can also be combined with other flowers, grasses, infructescence or leaves for stunning impact. The variety is infinite and also symbolises eternity and the diversity of life.

Rosenkränze in Pink

In Pink trumpft die Rose erst richtig auf. Für Kränze ein anziehender Blickfang, der in der Trauerhalle als Schmuck auf dem Sarg oder nach der Beerdigung auf dem frischen Grab einen auffälligen Akzent bildet.

Rose wreaths in pink

In shades of pink, roses really show what they are made of. Done up in wreaths they are appealing and yet consoling eye-catchers, providing a high-profile accent for the funeral parlour as a casket decoration or to adorn the gravesite after the funeral service.

Bunter Rosenkranz

In einem Deutungsversuch zur Symbolkraft der Rose werden ihre Blütenblätter mit Liedern verglichen, die zum Schlaf, zur Ruhe und zur Erlösung auffordern. Kann es demnach eine passendere Blume für einen Trauerkranz geben?

Rose wreath

In an attempt to interpret the symbolic power of the rose, its flower petals are compared to eyelids, beckoning to slumber, peace and redemption. Could there be a more fitting flower for a funeral wreath?

Herzensrose

Rote Rosen und Dornenzweige sind Symbole für Liebe, Leid und Erlösung. Die Kraft der Liebe aber überwindet alles. So zeigt sich die Hoffnung auf Leben von ihrer schönsten Seite.

Heart rose

Red roses and thorny twigs are symbols of love, sorrow and redemption. But the power of love conquers all. Here the hope of life shows itself from its best side.

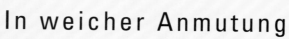

In weicher Anmutung

Die zarten Farben und die feingliedrige Struktur der Chrysanthemenblüten strahlen Ruhe aus und verleihen diesen Kränzen ihre liebreizende Gestalt.

In soft ambience

The delicate colours and intricate structure of the chrysanthemum flowers exude peace and give these wreaths their sweet and charming appearance.

Gepflanzter Sommergruß

Blüten, die weithin leuchten, Kräuter, die für Stärke, Liebe und Heil stehen und ihre würzigen Düfte verbreiten. Sommerkränze zeigen das Leben in seiner ganzen Fülle und tragen den Gedanken der Unsterblichkeit weiter.

Planted summer greeting

Flowers with very vivid colours, herbs that stand for strength, love and spiritual salvation and spread their heady scent. Summer wreaths show life in all its fullness and carry on the idea of immortality.

Stilvolle Exoten

Klassisch und doch ein wenig exotisch mutet das Kopfbouquet mit den Anthurien an. Kombiniert mit imposanten Blättern oder weißen Rosen ergibt sich ein harmonisches Gesamtbild.

Stylish exotics

Classic and yet a bit exotic is the wreath spray with Anthurium flowers. Combined with imposing leaves or white roses for a well-rounded harmonious design.

Zeichen ewigen Lebens

Blumen und Getreide als Zeichen für Lebendigkeit und Unsterblichkeit. Die leichte, sommerliche Anmutung macht diese Kränze zu Hoffnungsspendern.

Sign of everlasting life

Flowers and grain as symbols of vitality and immortality. The light, summery look turns these wreaths into sources of hope and faith.

Schlichte Eleganz

Schlicht und glatt anmutende Kränze aus Rhododendron- oder
Bergenienblättern kombiniert mit den warmen, sonnigen Farbtönen
des Spätsommers. Blüten und florale Ketten strahlen Hoffnung aus.

Simple elegance

Simple and smooth-looking wreaths of *Rhododendron* or *Bergenia*
leaves combined with the warm, sunny hues of late summer. Flowers
and floral chains radiate hope.

Rustikale Schönheit

Die Ausstrahlung dieses Kranzes ist aufgrund der gewählten
Materialien sehr naturnah. Aber trotz seiner eher bodenständigen
Erscheinung büßt er nichts an Würde ein.

Rustic beauty

Due to the choice of the material this wreath has a
very natural look. But despite its somewhat
uncomplicated and earthy design this wreath
is every bit as dignified.

Früchte des Lebens

So reichhaltig die Natur uns versorgt, so reichhaltig kann das Leben sein. Diese Kränze lassen hoffen und eignen sich für einen Menschen, der voller Lebensfreude war.

Fruit of life

As substantially as Mother Nature provides for us, just as generous can life itself be. These wreaths inspire hope and are very suitable for a person who, in life, was full of joie de vivre.

Physalis-Kranz

Ein Kranz, der durch seine Leichtigkeit, Transparenz und ungewöhnliche Materialzusammenstellung wirkt.

Physalis wreath

A wreath whose stunning impact is due to its lightness, transparency and unusual combination of materials.

Flair des Südens

Die Olive steht für Frieden und Unsterblichkeit. Die Kombination mit einer einzelnen weiße Lilie macht diesen Kranz so unvergleichlich.

Mediterranean flair

An olive branch or wreath stands for peace and immortality. The combination with a single white lily is what makes this wreath so incomparable.

Schlichter Charme

Ein Kranz, der durch seine Natürlichkeit und spröde Holzigkeit besticht. Clematisranken bilden die zurückhaltende Basis für die Lieblingsblume des Verstorbenen.

Simple charm

A wreath that appeals with its natural flair and brittle woodiness. *Clematis* vines provide a reserved basis for the favourite flower of the deceased.

Symbolhafte Efeuranken

Unsterblichkeit, ewiges Leben und Treue. Für all das steht der Efeu und bildet dadurch symbolträchtige Kränze, die mit wenig Gestaltung auskommen.

Symbolic ivy vines

Immortality, eternal life and loyalty. The ivy stands for all of this and is therefore ideal for making highly symbolic wreaths, which require little design technique.

Immerwährend

Ein schlichter Kranz aus immergrünem Ilex ist nicht nur aufgrund seiner Oberflächenstruktur besonders wirkungsvoll, er ist zudem auch überaus haltbar. Je nach Verwendung als Trauer- oder Gedenkkranz kann er pur oder mit einem natürlichen Schmuckakzent zum Einsatz kommen.

Everlasting

A simple wreath of evergreen *Ilex* is not only high-impact due to its interesting texture, it is also extremely long-lasting. Depending on whether its purpose is for a funeral or memorial wreath, it can be used on its own or with a natural decorative accent.

Feuerwerk der Farben

Golden kann der Herbst sein. Und sein unvergleichlicher Farben-reichtum bringt Lichtblicke, Wärme und die Hoffnung auf ein Leben nach dem Tod.

Fireworks of colour

Autumn can be so golden. And its wealth of colours brings highlights, warmth and the belief in a life after death.

Blättervielfalt

Farbenfroh gezeichnete Blätter und Heide im Kontrast. Diese gepflanzten Kränze sind eine Hommage an die Farben des Herbstes, die auch kälteren Tagen Stand hält.

Foliage diversity

Gaily-coloured leaves with interesting markings and heather in contrast. These planted wreaths are a homage to the colours of autumn, just the ticket for holding out against cold days.

Blüten
der kalten Jahreszeit

Ob die Urwüchsigkeit und Kraft des Waldes vermittelnd oder als
Zeichen für den unerschütterlichen Fortbestand der Natur. Diese
Kränze stellen sich tapfer kalten und traurigen Zeiten entgegen und
behalten ihre schmückende Wirkung bis zum Frühjahr.

Blossoms
of the cold season

Whether communicating the earthiness and energy of the forest or
as a symbol of the unshakeable, continuing existence of nature.
These wreaths stand up bravely to cold and dismal days and retain
their decorative effect until spring.

Blumen des Lichts

In dem dezent bepflanzten Kranz in Grün-Weiß blühen im Winter die Christrosen. Sie bringen Licht in eine Zeit der Trauer. Die verschiedenen Grau-Nuancen verleihen puristische Eleganz.

Flowers of light

The subdued, planted wreath in green-and-white will sprout Christmas roses throughout the winter. They bring light to a time of mourning. The various grey nuances lend a touch of purist elegance.

Gedenkavantgarde

Weiß steht für Reinheit und ist eine symbolträchtige Farbe in der Trauerfloristik. Auch eine moderne Gestaltung kann für „Ewigkeit" stehen, wie der außergewöhnliche Lunaria-Kranz zeigt.

Remembrance avant-garde

White stands for purity and is a highly symbolic colour in funeral design. A modern creation can also stand for "eternity", for example as this extraordinary Lunaria wreath demonstrates.

Band und Text am Kranz

Schleifenbänder finden sich üblicherweise am Werkstück Kranz. Das Textile stellt nicht nur gestalterisch eine Akzentuierung dar, es bietet darüber hinaus die Möglichkeit, mit einem entsprechenden Aufdruck einen kurzen Abschiedsgruß zu formulieren. Hier bieten sich verschiedene Verfahren an:

1. Das Heißprägeverfahren. Dabei werden einzelne Prägebuchstaben mit Hilfe von Hitze auf eine Kranzbandschleife übertragen. Die Buchstaben wirken plastisch und wertig. Die Art der Buchstaben ist begrenzt, dafür ist das Bedrucken in Gold und Silber möglich. Manchmal besteht die Gefahr, dass sich die Klebebuchstaben leicht vom Untergrund lösen.

2. Das Computerdruckverfahren. Dabei wird die Kranzschleife über einen PC mit angeschlossenem Drucker bedruckt. Das Kranzschleifenband muss eine relativ glatte Oberfläche aufweisen, vor allem Satin- und Acetatbänder sind geeignet. Der Vorteil dieses Verfahrens liegt in der flexibel anpassbaren Textgröße und Schriftart. Das Bedrucken mit metallischen Farben ist nicht möglich. Die Texte sollten anschließend mit einem Fixierspray haltbar gemacht werden, damit diese nicht durch Feuchtigkeit, zum Beispiel während der Kühllagerung oder draußen im Freien bei feuchtem Wetter, verwischen.

3. Die Handbeschriftung. Dabei wird der textile Untergrund von Hand mit Pinsel und entsprechender Farbe beschriftet. Handmaler gibt es nur noch in wenigen Gegenden. Insofern wird dieses schönste, flexibelste und wertigste Verfahren aufgrund fehlenden Nachwuchses nicht mehr lange möglich sein.

4. Das Besticken. Auch das Besticken von Kranzschleifen gibt es nur noch in wenigen Gegenden, weil es nur noch wenige Maschinen gibt. Es ist das teuerste, aber auch das haltbarste Verfahren, weil sich der Text direkt mit dem Bandmaterial verbindet.

Ribbon and inscriptions

Many funeral wreaths are adorned with ribbons and bows. This textile component not only represents an accentuation, but also offers the possibility of formulating a short farewell message in printed form. There are several options for doing this:

1. Hot foil blocking. Here the individual embossing letters are transferred to the ribbon banner by applying heat. The letters have a three-dimensional and high-quality look. Although the type of lettering is limited, it can be done in gold and silver. Sometimes there is the danger of the hot-glued letters falling off the substrate.

2. Computer printing. Here the banner is printed on a PC with a connected printer. For this method, the ribbon must have a fairly smooth surface texture, so particularly satin and acetate ribbons are suitable. The advantage of this method lies in the flexibility of the many font sizes and typefaces. Printing with metallic inks, however is not possible. The lettering should be set with a fixing spray after printing, so that it doesn't smudge when exposed to moisture, for example during cold storage or outside in wet weather.

3. Hand painting. Here the letters are painted by hand right on the textile substrate with a paintbrush and suitable paint. Unfortunately there are no longer many hand painters around.

4. Embroidery. Here again, the embroidery of wreath banners is an art that is dying out as there aren't many machines left. It is the most expensive, but at the same time longest-lasting method, as the lettering is directly connected to the ribbon material.

Dekorative Bandenden

Edle Satin-, Moiré- oder Acetat-bänder erhalten durch indivi-duelle Bandabschlüsse eine zusätzliche Aufwertung. Meist werden die Bänder einfach mit der Schere geschnitten, wo-durch diese Schnittenden leicht ausfransen. Durch das Aufbrin-gen von handelsüblichen Kor-deln, Fransenbändern oder Zier-nähten kann dies umgangen werden. Außerdem kann der Florist durch das Aufkleben floraler Materialien hier einen zusätzlichen Schmuck schaffen. Mit Halmen, Blättern oder getrockneten Blüten lassen sich so die Kanten individuell und passend zum Kranz oder Werkstück gestalten. Es ist meist nur ein kleiner Mehraufwand, der dafür aber große Wirkung erzielt.

Ribbon finishing

You can make a bit more of fancy satin, moiré and acetate ribbons by adding customised facings on the cut ends. Most of the time ribbons are simply cut with scissors, and the cut edge allowed to fray a bit. Dressing them up with commercially bought cords, fringed ribbon or decorative stitching will solve this problem. Additionally, the florist can create extra embellishments by gluing on floral materials along the edge. This way, with grass blades, leaves or dried flowers the edge can be designed individually and in line with the wreath or assembly. Usually it's only a bit more work, but the additional impact is well worth it.

MORS
PORTA
VITAE

Abschied in Dankbarkeit

Farewell in eternal
gratitude

Wie die Zeit vergeht

As time goes by

EIN ENGEL GEHT AUF REISEN

An angel departs from
our midst

Aus Gottes Hand - in Gottes Hand

God giveth and He
taketh away

Der erste Schritt in die Ewigkeit

The first step to ever-
lasting life

Es ist Zeit.
Unsere Gedanken
gehen mit Dir.

Your time has come. Our
thoughts are with you.

Es kam der Abend und
ich tauchte in die Sterne

My heart rests on the night's
velvet and stars lie down on my
eyelids

GELIEBT UND
UNVERGESSEN

In loving memory

Hab Dank
für Deine Liebe

Your love meant so much

Mein Ziel ist
hinter aller Zeit

Rest in peace

Der Tod ist das Tor zum Leben

Danke

Die Liebe ist größer als der Tod

Our refuge and strength

IN JEDEM ENDE STEHT EIN ANFANG

In every ending is a new beginning

Durch den Tod zum Leben

Whosoever believeth in the Son hath everlasting life

VERBUNDEN ÜBER DEN TOD HINAUS

Forever united in love

Du bleibst in unseren Herzen

You will always be in our hearts

In Liebe verbunden über den Tod hinaus

Forever united in a love beyond death

In unserem Herzen lebst Du weiter

Forever in our hearts

STÄRKER ALS DER TOD IST DIE LIEBE

Love is stronger than death

Von der Erde gegangen, im Herzen geblieben

Departed from this Earth but forever in our earts

Was man nicht aufgibt, hat man nicht verloren

Sorrow is brief but joy is endless

DER TOD IST DIE PFORTE ZUM LEBEN

Death is but a gateway to everlasting life

Kränze nach klassischem Vorbild

Der klassische Römer wurde aus Lorbeerblättern gestaltet. Moderne Varianten setzen die Fülle der Blattformen und -strukturen auf ähnlich pure und elegant-klassische Weise ein.

Wreath with a classic model

The classic wreath – originating in ancient Rome – was made of bay or laurel leaves. Modern variations use a host of leaf shapes and structures in a similarly pure and elegant classic design.

Rote Blattkränze

Die klassischen Blattkränze müssen nicht nur aus grünen Blättern gestaltet sein. Besondere Ausstrahlung haben die violetten Blätter einiger Stauden und Gehölze. Von links nach rechts: *Heuchera, Galax, Fagus sylvatica,* gefülltes *Galax*-Blatt.

Wreath with red foliage

Classic foliage wreaths don't necessarily have to be made of green leaves. Special effects can be achieved with the violet leaves of many perennials and shrubs. From left to right: *Heuchera, Galax, Fagus sylvatica,* rolled *Galax* leaf.

Eleganz und Würde in Violettrot

Schlichte, ruhige Blattkränze können zusätzlich mit einem Band oder mit Blüten geschmückt werden – ganz nach Belieben. Diese aus violettroten Blättern gestalteten Blattkränze zeigen die Vielfalt der Möglichkeiten.

Elegance and dignity in violet-red

Simple, regular-shaped foliage wreaths can be further adorned with a ribbon or a spray of flowers – it's all a matter of personal taste. These foliage wreaths of violet-red leaves demonstrate the wide range of possible ideas.

207

GESTECKE BASED TRIBUTES

Sommerlich
mit Blütenfülle

Eine Vielzahl sommerlicher Blüten gruppiert sich um eine üppige Schleife, die der Blickpunkt der farbenfrohen Grabgestecke ist.

Summery tribute
with masses of flowers

Lots of summery flowers in clusters surround a luxurious ribbon banner, which is always the focal point of colourful based tributes.

Buketts in Rosé

Die Farbe Rosé steht für einen wertigen und repräsentativen Ausdruck. Im Blumenbereich wird sie von vielen Blüten getragen und unterstreicht im Gesteck diskrete Verbundenheit und Würdigung des Verstorbenen.

Bouquets in rosé

The colour pink stands for a significant and distinguished expression of sympathy. Carried by many of the flowers in the arrangement, underscoring the feelings of closeness and respect for the deceased.

Blütenkissen
mit Kreuzsymbolik

Das Kreuz als christliches Symbol der Hoffnung und Auferstehung ist Bestandteil aller Blütenkissen. Diese können quadratisch, rechteckig oder in gestreckter, länglicher Form gestaltet sein.

Floral cushion
with cross symbol

The cross as a Christian symbol of hope and resurrection is a component of all floral cushions and pillows. These can be designed in a rectangular, square or more elongated shape.

ZEIT FÜR TRÄNEN

Rund mit Mitte
aus tausend Blüten

Immer wird die blütenreiche Mitte umkränzt. Sei es durch grüne Blätter und Rankenschlingungen, durch einen Graskranz oder eingesteckte Nelken und Efeublätter. Diese runden Buketts sind handlich und leicht und sollten deshalb auf dem Grab mit einem Holzsplint fest auf der Erde verankert werden.

Posy pad
with a thousand blooms

In every posy the masses of flowers in the centre are encircled, either by green leaves and tendrils of vines, a grass edge or a ring of based carnations and ivy. These round bouquets are lightweight and easy to carry and should therefore be secured on the grave with a wooden pick.

Grabgestecke
in Symbolformen

Kissen, Herzen oder Kreuze. Alle diese Formen für Blütengestecke sind Zeichen der Ruhe, Liebe und Auferstehung. Besonders zu Gedenktagen kann mit solch einem Blumenschmuck auf dem Grab an den Verstorbenen erinnert werden: zu seinem Geburtstag, zum Hochzeitstag oder zu einem anderen sehr persönlichen Anlass.

Based tributes
in symbolic shapes

Cushions, hearts or crosses. All of these shapes for based assemblies are symbols of peace, love and resurrection. Especially on a day of remembrance, such floral decorations on the grave of a loved one can mark a birthday, wedding anniversary or other very personal occasion.

Blütenherzen mono

Blütenherzen, überwiegend aus den gleichen Blumen oder Ton-in-Ton besteckt, bestechen durch ihre Klarheit und besondere Ausstrahlung. Sie eignen sich nicht nur für den Abschied von einem geliebten Menschen, sondern sind auch ganz persönliche Ausdrucksformen für das Grab anlässlich eines Gedenktages.

Floral hearts in mono

Floral hearts, usually massed with a single kind of flower or based tone-in-tone, have special impact due to their clarity and special aura. They are suitable not only as a last farewell to a much-loved person, but also as a highly personal form of expression for the grave on the occasion of a personal day of remembrance.

Blütenherzen
bunt und fröhlich

Auch bunte Blütenherzen sind ein würdiger und gleichzeitig optimis-
tischer Abschiedsgruß, der von Herzen kommt. Rosen stehen dabei
für innigliche Liebe, der bunte Sommerflor für die Erinnerung an viele
frohe, gemeinsame Stunden.

Gaily-coloured floral heart

Colourful floral hearts are a dignified and at the same time optimistic
farewell tribute that comes from the heart. Roses stand for deep and
sincere love, while the bright summer flora is a reminder of many
happy hours spent together in life.

Klassische Blütenkissen

Die rechteckigen, nahezu quadratischen Blütenkissen sind die üblichen, handlichen Gestecke für den Schmuck eines Grabes. Sie lassen sich mit fast allen Blüten bestecken, der Frischsteckschaum garantiert eine lange Blütenfrische.

Classic floral cushions

Symbolic of eternal rest, square cushions or more rectangular floral pillows are a very popular based tribute for decorating a grave. They can be massed with almost any type of flowers, and the floral foam base guarantees long-lasting freshness.

Sommerliches Blütenkissen

Aus nur zwei Blütenarten ist dieses in warmen Tönen gehaltene Blütenkissen gestaltet. Alstroemeria unterstreichen liebevoll zurückhaltend die eleganten Rosen, die dem Kissen die entscheidende Wirkung verleihen.

Floral cushion in summer hues

A floral pillow with only two varieties of flowers in warm tones. With affectionate reserve the Alstroemeria lilies underscore the elegant roses, which for their part give the cushion its undeniable impact.

Natürliche Blütenkissen

Auch Ton-in-Ton haben die Blütenkissen ihren Reiz. Selbst das grüne Gras wirkt dekorativ und interessant, wenn es durch einige besondere Blumen, möglichst ebenfalls in Grün-Weiß, ergänzt wird.

Natural floral cushion

Designing a floral pillow tone-in-tone also creates special charm. Even the green grass adds decorative and interesting flair when it is supplemented by a few special flowers, also predominantly in green and white.

Aprikotfarbene
Blütengestecke

Nelken, Chrysanthemen oder Rosen, die Blumen, die gerne in trauer-
floristischen Gebinden eingesetzt werden, weisen eine breite
Palette an Farben auf. So auch Aprikot oder die Lachsfarbe, die
Grabgestecken eine dezente, würdige Ausstrahlung verleiht.

Based tributes
in apricot

Carnations, chrysanthemums and roses, the flowers often used
in funeral design, encompass a wide spectrum of colours. For
example, apricot or salmon, shades that lend such based tributes
a subdued and dignified air.

Blütenkugeln
mit Bandschmuck

Die Kugel als die vollkommene Form bildet hier die Grundlage der blütenreichen Grabschmuckteile. Band ist jedes Mal als Akzent eingearbeitet, entweder als eigene, mittig platzierte Kugelform, die Blütengestaltung durchziehend oder wie eine Manschette umhüllend.

Floral ball with ribbons

The sphere as a symbol of completeness forms the basis for these massed floral tributes. In each case ribbons are integrated into the assemblies, either as an additional, centrally-placed ball, weaving its way among the florals or forming a frill around the assembly.

Spannungsreiche Dreiecke

Strukturiert und spannungsvoll sind diese auffälligen Grabgestecke in Dreiecksform gestaltet. Sie werden damit zu Interesse weckenden Schmuckakzenten für Gräber, die eher zurückhaltend und gleichförmig bepflanzt oder belegt sind.

Triangles with impact

Very structured and with plenty of impact, these eye-catching based tributes are done in the shape of a triangle. This is sure to make fascinating decorations for graves that are otherwise adorned with reserved and plain plants.

Helle Blütengestecke

Blütenschmuck in hellen Farben hebt sich gut vor den meist dunkleren Grabflächen ab. Vor allem in trüben Monaten ist dies ein tröstlicher Akzent auf dem Friedhof.

Pale floral tributes

Floral decorations in pale shades make a lovely contrast to the mostly darkish grave surfaces. Especially in overcast months they make a consoling accent at the cemetery.

Blütengestecke mit Bandschmuck

Auch Formgestecke wie Blütenherzen lassen sich zusätzlich mit einem Schleifenband akzentuieren. Vor allem dann, wenn sie aus einer einzigen Blumensorte oder farblich Ton-in-Ton gestaltet wurden, was einen weiteren Akzent zulässt. Über ein bedrucktes Dekorationsband ist die Übermittlung einer Botschaft möglich, was die persönliche Würdigung des Verstorbenen verstärkt.

Based tributes with banners

Even symbolic floral hearts can be additionally accented with a banner. This looks especially good if the flowers are all the same kind or colour, which allows for an extra highlight. A custom printed banner makes it possible to add a personal message, which further emphasises the personal respect for the deceased.

Schärpe handbeschriftet
Zu dem gleichmäßigen und zurückhaltend in Grün-Weiß-Creme gestalteten Blütenherz passt sehr gut eine breite, quer verlaufende Schärpe aus cremefarbenem Kranzschleifenband. Die Schrift ist von Hand mit einem wasserfesten Goldstift aufgebracht worden.

Hand-written sash script
On the evenly massed and minimalist green-white-cream floral heart a wide diagonally positioned sash of cream-coloured ribbon looks especially good. The script is written on the ribbon by hand with a permanent gold marker.

Farbiger Trauerflor
Asymmetrisch lässt sich auch ein Trauerflor am Herz anbringen. Das schwarze Transparentband wird zusammen mit der cremegelben Kranzschleife an einen Steckdraht geknotet und vorsichtig zwischen den Blüten auf der Unterlage befestigt.

Coloured mourning crepe
A mourning crepe can also be positioned asymmetrically across a floral heart. The black transparent ribbon is knotted together with the cream yellow banner to a stub wire and attached carefully between the flowers to the base.

SERVICE SERVICE

Die Nelken werden dicht an dicht zusammengenommen und unterm Kopf gebunden. Schleierkraut wird umgelegt und gebunden. Dann *Tillandsia* mit Silberdraht umwickeln, so dass die konische Form entsteht. Nun *Laurus*-Blätter mit Dekonadeln feststecken und die Nelkenstiele mit Steelgras ummanteln.

The carnations are bunched together in a compact bouquet and tied just below the calyx. A halo of baby's breath is then arranged around the bouquet and secured. Next the *Tillandsia* is wound about with silver wire to make a cone-shaped structure. Finally, the *Laurus* leaves are attached with decorative pins and the stems of the carnations are covered with stalks of bear grass.

Auf eine Tütenunterlage aus Pappe wird mit Sprühkleber schwarzes Papier geklebt. Die Kanten nach innen umschlagen und Kreuzform aus Steelgras mit Kaltkleber aufbringen.

With spray glue affix black paper to a card base. Fold the edges under and glue on a cross symbol of bear grass.

1 Oberen Teil einer Steckschaum-kugel aushöhlen, um die Urne hier später aufsetzen zu können. Den unteren Teil abschneiden, um eine sichere Standfläche zu erhalten.
1 Scoop out the upper section of a floral foam sphere, so that you can fit the urn inside later. Slice off the bottom to make a flat, secure base to stand the arrangement.

2 Das untere Drittel der vorbereiteten Kugel wird mit Efeuranken umlegt, das spart Blüten und gibt eine frische Wirkung.
2 The lower section of the prepared sphere is based with ivy vines. This saves on flowers while creating a look of freshness.

SEITE 59
Ummantelung
Aristea africana, Ceropegia woodii, Phalaenopsis, Piper

PAGE 59
Encirclement
Aristea africana, Ceropegia woodii, Phalaenopsis, Piper

SEITE 60
Florale Halbkugel
Steckunterlage, *Dianthus caryophyllus, Gerbera jamesonii, Helleborus orientale, Hypericum Cultivar, Ranunculus asiaticus, Tillandsia usneoides, Viburnum opulus, Viburnum tinus*

PAGE 60
Floral semi-sphere
floral foam sphere, *Dianthus caryophyllus, Gerbera jamesonii, Helleborus orientale, Hypericum cultivar, Ranunculus asiaticus, Tillandsia usneoides, Viburnum opulus, Viburnum tinus*

SEITE 61
Blütenkissen
Steckunterlage, *Chrysanthemum Cultivar, Fritillaria meleagris, Gerbera jamesonii, Viburnum opulus, Rosa Cultivar, Viburnum opulus, Viburnum tenax*

PAGE 61
Floral cushion
floral foam base, *Chrysanthemum cultivar, Fritillaria meleagris, Gerbera jamesonii, Viburnum opulus, Rosa cultivar, Viburnum opulus, Viburnum tenax*

SEITE 61
Blütenherz
Bergenia Cultivar, Cornus mas, Muehlenbeckia axillaris, Muscari armeniacum, Skimmia japonica, Ranunculus asiaticus, Rosa Cultivar, Trockengestrüpp

PAGE 61
Floral heart
Bergenia cultivar, Cornus mas, Muehlenbeckia axillaris, Muscari armeniacum, Skimmia japonica, Ranunculus asiaticus, Rosa cultivar, dried brushwood

Aus abgespultem Wickeldraht wird ein Herz geformt, das innen hohl und offen ist. Trockene, grasartige Werkstoffe werden hier als Basis eingewebt und die *Cornus*-Zweige Halt gebend eingesteckt, bevor die Blüten ohne weitere Wasserversorgung hinzugefügt werden.

A heart is moulded of reel wire, leaving inside a hollow and open space. Dried grasses and vines are woven in through the spaces between the wires to form the basis and then the *Cornus* twigs are inserted for added stability, before the flowers are added without a built-in water supply.

SEITE 62/63
Urnengalerie
Links: *Buxus sempervirens, Cotinus coggygria, Dianthus barbatus, Gypsophila elegans, Heuchera-*Blätter, *Hydrangea macrophylla*
Mitte: *Ammi majus, Euphorbia amygdaloides, Helleborus niger-*Fruchtstände, *Rosa Cultivar, Myrtus communis*
Rechts: *Senecio bicolor, Stachys byzantina-*Blätter, *Tillandsia usneoides*

PAGE 62/63
Urn gallery
left: *Buxus sempervirens, Cotinus coggygria, Dianthus barbatus, Gypsophila elegans, Heuchera* leaves, *Hydrangea macrophylla*
centre: *Ammi majus, Euphorbia amygdaloides, Helleborus niger* inflorescence, *Rosa cultivar, Myrtus communis*
right: *Senecio bicolor, Stachys byzantina* leaves, *Tillandsia usneoides*

Die Präsentationskissen aus Trockensteckschaum werden in die gewünschte Form geschnitten, entweder Karo oder Raute, und dann mit den Floralien versehen. Teilweise können diese geklebt, teilweise gehaftet werden.

The presentation pillows of floral foam are trimmed to the desired shape, either square or diamond-shaped, and then the florals are arranged on the foam. In some cases they are glued, otherwise they are pushed firmly into the foam.

SEITE 64
Umkränzungen
Links: *Equisetum palustre, Rosa Cultivar*
Rechts: *Alchemilla mollis, Myrtus communis, Rosa Cultivar*

PAGE 64
Urn wreaths
left: *Equisetum palustre, Rosa cultivar*
right: *Alchemilla mollis, Myrtus communis, Rosa cultivar*

SEITE 65
Urne mit Schilfflechtung
*Asparagus-*Ranke, *Cynara scolymus, Passiflora-*Ranke, Schilfflechtband, *Viburnum rhytidophyllum*

PAGE 65
Urn with woven reed band
left: *Asparagus* vine, *Cynara scolymus, Passiflora* vine, woven reed band, *Viburnum rhytidophyllum*

SEITE 66
Gewundenes Kränzchen
Asparagus asparagoides, Buxus sempervirens, Calocephalus brownii, Hamamelis mollis, Hedera helix, Paeonia, Rosa Cultivar, Viburnum opulus

PAGE 66
Wound wreath
Asparagus asparagoides, Buxus sempervirens, Calocephalus brownii, Hamamelis mollis, Hedera helix, Paeonia, Rosa cultivar, Viburnum opulus

SEITE 67
Säulengestaltung
*Acacia dealbata, Cornus-*Zweige, *Stephanotis floribunda, Zantedeschia Cultivar,* trockene „Kissen-*Euphorbie*", Weidenband

PAGE 67
Pillar design
Acacia dealbata, Cornus twigs, *Stephanotis floribunda, Zantedeschia cultivar,* dried cushion *Euphorbia,* wicker mat

Das Weidenband wird mit *Cornus-*Zweigen durchsteckt und durchflochten. Das gibt Stabilität. Die Blüten werden dann durch das grobmaschige Geflecht geführt und mit Draht fixiert.

The wicker mat is further stabilised by inserting and interweaving *Cornus* twigs through it. Then the flowers are arranged in the loose spaces of the mat and affixed with wires.

SEITE 68
Farbige Akzentuierung
Links: *Galax urceolata, Hedera helix, Muehlenbeckia axillaris, Ranunculus asiaticus*
Rechts: *Equisetum pallustre, Eucalyptus gunnii, Strelitzia reginae*

PAGE 68
Colour accent
left: *Galax urceolata, Hedera helix, Muehlenbeckia axillaris, Ranunculus asiaticus*
right: *Equisetum pallustre, Eucalyptus gunnii, Strelitzia reginae*

SEITE 69
Umkränzungen klassisch
Buxus sempervirens, Rosa Cultivar, Trockenranken

Aus Wickeldraht wird ein flaches
Band hergestellt.

Wrapping wire is moulded into a
flat band.

Dieses Drahtband wird über einen
gewässerten und auf einem Brett
befestigten Steckschaumblock
gebogen.

A soaked block of floral foam,
affixed to a block of wood, is
inserted inside the wire netting.

Durch das Drahtgewirr zuerst
formgebende *Cornus*-Zweige, anschließend die Blüten einstecken.

Through the spaces between
the wires insert sturdy *Cornus*
branches to create the outline,
then fill in the remaining gaps
with flowers.

Aus Wickeldraht wird ein langes
Rechteck geformt und mit Weiden-
zweigen längs und quer an den
Seiten und am Boden verstärkt.
Einige Zweige ragen aus der
Form heraus.

A long rectangular structure is
moulded of wrapping wire and
reinforced with a criss-cross of
wicker sticks along the sides and
bottom. A few branches are
allowed to protrude from the
basic outline.

In die lockere Grundform wird ein
Stück Stoff eingefügt, um den Sarg
vor der Blumenerde zu schützen.

In the loose basic structure a strip
of rough fabric is inserted to pro-
tect the casket from soiling by the
potting soil.

Die Wurzelballen der Pflanzen werden mit Moos umwickelt und Draht befestigt. Dabei mit dem Draht durch den Ballen stechen und so die Pflanze an der Grundkonstruktion fixieren.

The root balls of the plants are wrapped in moss and secured with wires. Through each of the balls a stay wire is inserted and then affixed firmly to the new 'basket'.

SEITE 88/89
Blütenwolke
Steckunterlage, *Ageratum houstonianum, Anemone Cultivar, Galax urceolata, Gerbera jamesonii, Gypsophila paniculata, Lilium longiflorum, Rosa Cultivar*

PAGE 88/89
Floral cloud
floral foam base, *Ageratum houstonianum, Anemone cultivar, Galax urceolata, Gerbera jamesonii, Gypsophila paniculata, Lilium longiflorum, Rosa cultivar*

Wie bei einem Fries eine lange Holzlatte mit Steckschaum vorbereiten. Erst seitlich das Schleierkraut einstecken, dann Blumen und Blätter auf der oberen Fläche in gleichmäßiger Höhe hinzufügen.

Like a frieze a long wooden board is fitted with floral foam. To begin the baby's breath is inserted from the sides, then the flowers and leaves are added along the top, keeping a uniform height.

SEITE 90/91
Flach besteckter Blütendeckel
Steckunterlage, *Achillea filipendulina, Astrantia major, Dianthus caryophyllus, Hydrangea macrophylla, Lathyrus odoratus, Limonium latifolium, Pelargonium, Rosa Cultivar, Scabiosa columbaria,* Kräuter, Gräser

PAGE 90/91
Flat floral casket arrangement
floral foam base, *Achillea filipendulina, Astrantia major, Dianthus caryophyllus, Hydrangea macrophylla, Lathyrus odoratus, Limonium latifolium, Pelargonium, Rosa cultivar, Scabiosa columbaria,* herbs, grasses

SEITE 92/93
Gesteck in Sommerfarben
Steckunterlage, *Alchemilla mollis, Amaranthus caudatus, Aster ericoides, Asparagus setaceus, Asparagus virgatus, Delphinium ajacis, Eustoma grandiflorum, Limonium ferulaceum, Ophiopogon grandis, Paeonia suffruticosa, Rosa Cultivar, Rudbeckia hirta, Scabiosa atropurpurea, Scabiosa caucasica,* Ranken

PAGE 92/93
Casket spray in summer hues
floral foam, *Alchemilla mollis, Amaranthus caudatus, Aster ericoides, Asparagus setaceus, Asparagus virgatus, Delphinium ajacis, Eustoma grandiflorum, Limonium ferulaceum, Ophiopogon grandis, Paeonia suffruticosa, Rosa Cultivar, Rudbeckia hirta, Scabiosa atropurpurea, Scabiosa caucasica,* vines

SEITE 94/95
Pyramidales Blütengesteck
Steckunterlage, *Antirrhinum majus, Aster ericoides, Astilbe Cultivar, Briza maxima, Bupleurum folium, Delphinium ajacis, Geranium, Gladiolus Cultivar, Gypsophila paniculata, Hippocrepis comosa, Hosta fortunei, Miscanthus sinensis, Paeonia lactiflora, Rosa Cultivar, Solidago, Tanacetum parthenium*

PAGE 94/95
Pyramidal floral spray
floral foam base, *Antirrhinum majus, Aster ericoides, Astilbe cultivar, Briza maxima, Bupleurum folium, Delphinium ajacis, Geranium, Gladiolus cultivar, Gypsophila paniculata, Hippocrepis comosa, Hosta fortunei, Miscanthus sinensis, Paeonia lactiflora, Rosa cultivar, Solidago, Tanacetum parthenium*

SEITE 96
Rosenspirale
Asparagus myriocladus, Asparagus setaceus, Rosa Cultivar, Ranken

PAGE 96
Rose spiral
Asparagus myriocladus, Asparagus setaceus, Rosa cultivar, vines

SEITE 97
Gesteck mit Blutbuchenzweigen
Amaranthus caudatus, Euphorbia polychroma, Fagus sylvatica `Atropurpurea`, Fritillaria persica, Rosa Cultivar, Gräser

PAGE 97
Spray with red beech branches
Amaranthus caudatus, Euphorbia polychroma, Fagus sylvatica `Atropurpurea`, Fritillaria persica, Rosa cultivar, grasses

SEITE 98/99
Rosengesteck in Dunkelrot
Steckunterlage, *Geranium, Hedera helix, Helleborus viridis, Heuchera, Hypericum calycinum, Rosa Cultivar*

PAGE 98/99
Rose tribute in dark-red
floral foam base, *Geranium, Hedera helix, Helleborus viridis, Heuchera, Hypericum calycinum, Rosa cultivar*

SEITE 100/101
Rosenblüten-Dreieck
Steckunterlage, *Rosa Cultivar, Viburnum rhytidophyllum*

PAGE 100/101
Rose petal triangle
floral foam base, *Rosa cultivar, Viburnum rhytidophyllum*

SEITE 102/103
Kranz als Ewigkeitssymbol
Gewundener Kranz aus: *Bistorta affinis, Clematis vitalba, Kerria japonica, Phormium tenax, Rosa Cultivar*

PAGE 102/103
The wreath as a symbol of eternity
winding wreath of: *Bistorta affinis, Clematis vitalba, Kerria japonica, Phormium tenax, Rosa cultivar*

SEITE 104
Kranzauflage
Fagus sylvatica `Atropurpurea`, Rosa Cultivar, Stephanotis floribunda

PAGE 104
Wreath tribute
Fagus sylvatica `Atropurpurea`, Rosa cultivar, Stephanotis floribunda

SEITE 105
Blaugoldener Linienschmuck
Kranzunterlage, *Bistorta affinis, Delphinium cultorum, Kerria japonica, Passiflora caerulea, Phormium tenax*

PAGE 105
Blue-and-gold lifeline
wreath base, *Bistorta affinis, Delphinium cultorum, Kerria japonica, Passiflora caerulea, Phormium tenax*

SEITE 106/107
Girlandenschmuck
Alchemilla mollis, Buxus sempervirens, Dianthus caryophyllus, Gypsophila paniculata

PAGE 106/107
Garland decoration
Alchemilla mollis, Buxus sempervirens, Dianthus caryophyllus, Gypsophila paniculata

SEITE 108
Asymmetrischer Calla-Bogen
Steckunterlage, *Asparagus asparagoides, Asparagus plumosus, Asparagus setaceus, Zantedeschia aethiopica*

PAGE 108
Asymmetrical Calla sheaf
floral foam base, *Asparagus asparagoides, Asparagus plumosus, Asparagus setaceus, Zantedeschia aethiopica*

SEITE 109
Stufensymbolik mit Rankenschmuck
Asparagus asparagoides, Asparagus plumosus, Asparagus setaceus, Galax urceolata, Physalis alkekengi, Rosa Cultivar

PAGE 109
Seven step symbolism with decorative vines
Asparagus asparagoides, Asparagus plumosus, Asparagus setaceus, Galax urceolata, Physalis alkekengi, Rosa cultivar

SEITE 110
Farbenfrohes Sargkreuz
Dendrobium Cultivar, Rosa Cultivar, Vanda Cultivar, Früchte, Geäst

PAGE 110
Colourful casket cross
Dendrobium cultivar, Rosa cultivar, Vanda cultivar, fruit, branches

SEITE 111
Rosenkreuz
Hedera helix, Cornus mas, Rosa Cultivar, Polygonum-Ranken

PAGE 111
Rose cross
Hedera helix, Cornus mas, Rosa cultivar, Polygonum vines

Aus Bambusstäben wird die überstreckte Kreuzform zurecht gelegt und die Stäbe an den Kreuzungspunkten mit Draht verbunden.

Bamboo rods form the basis for this elongated cross; the crossbars are lashed together with wires.

Die *Polygonum*-Ranken werden locker auf die Grundform gelegt und mit Wickeldraht befestigt.

The *Polygonum* vines are laid out loosely on the bamboo structure and secured with wrapping wire.

Mit den *Cornus*-Zweigen wird das Kreuz stabilisiert. Die Rosen werden dann im Kreuzmuster auf die Zweige geklemmt und mit *Polygonum*-Ranken überzogen.

The cross is then stabilised with *Cornus* branches. The roses are attached to the branches in a cross pattern and covered with criss-crosses of *Polygonum*.

Für die Spiralen mehrere der weichen und biegsamen Seitentriebe von *Salix* zu dünnen Ruten zusammen nehmen und mit Wickeldraht umwickeln.

For the spirals bundle several soft and flexible side shoots of *Salix* together and wrap in binding wire.

Aus den Ruten eine Spirale oder Schnecke drehen und zur Stabilisierung im mittleren Bereich und am Ende quer mit Wickeldraht fixieren.

Wind the rods into a spiral or snail shape and secure across the middle and at the end with binding wire.

Mit Efeunadeln (Haften) am Kranz befestigen.

Secure to the wreath with floral pins (greening pins).

Die Blätter werden am unteren
Ende mit Haften auf die Unterlage
genadelt. Eine Hafte pro Blatt
reicht bei diesem stabilen
Werkstoff.

The base of the leaves can easily
be pinned to the wreath form with
greening pins. One u-shaped pin
per leaf is sufficient with such a
sturdy material.

Auf Peddigrohr zieht man etwa 10
Früchte der Lampionblume zu einer
Kette auf.

String about 10 Chinese lantern
seedpods on a strip of rattan to
make a chain.

Für den Kranzkörper werden einzelne Stücke Peddigrohr locker
gewunden und durch Kabelbinder
verbunden. In die Windungen werden die Peddigrohrstücke mit den
Lampions eingezogen.

For the wreath form, individual
strips of rattan are loosely
wound and secured to one
another with cable ties. The
chains of seedpods are inserted
inside the loops in crosswise
rows.

Der so entstandene Kranz kann
durch wenige Kabelbinder-
Bahnen, die im Ring mitlaufen,
gefestigt werden. Eine transparen-
te, leichte Form ist entstanden.

When the ring is filled with rows
of seedpods the wreath is
complete. A few rows of cable
ties, running along the ring, give
added security. Thus a transparent, light wreath form is created.

Clematis in sich zu einem Kranz
winden und mit Wickeldraht
fixieren. Zwischen die Schich-
tungen mit Hilfe von Glasröhr-
chen die Blumen und Blätter
einstecken. Wer von vorne herein
haltbare Floralien wählt, kann auf
die Wasserversorgung mittels
Wasserröhrchen verzichten.

Intertwine the *Clematis* vines into
a wreath and secure with wire.
Between the layers insert flowers
and foliage in tiny glass tubes.
If lasting florals are to be used,
no glass tubes will be required
for supplying water.

Frische Blumen – wie beispiels-
weise *Scabiosa* – werden in den
unteren Schichten mit Glasröhr-
chen eingearbeitet.

Fresh flowers – for example
Scabiosa – are integrated in the
lower layers in tiny glass tubes.

Die Basis bildet ein dünner Ring
aus Weidenruten, der mit den
langen Efeuranken umwunden
wird. Vereinzelt werden die
Ranken mit geglühtem Wickeldraht an der Unterlage befestigen.
Wichtig ist, dass die Ranken
locker aufeinander liegen, der
Umriss muss eine klare, gleichmäßig breite Kranzform erken-
nen lassen.

The base is a thin ring of wicker
rods, which are intertwined with
the ivy vines. The vines are
individually secured to the wreath
base with annealed stub wire.
Important: the vines should lie
loosely over one another, and the
outline must demonstrate a clear,
even-width wreath form.

Auf einige Blätter wird mit Hilfe
von Sprühkleber Schlagmetall
aufgetragen.

Silver leaf is adhered to some of
the leaves with the help of spray
glue.

Ein Strohrömer dient als Unterlage,
auf dem die Blätter des *Ilex* kreuz
und quer mit Stecknadeln gesteckt
sind. Wichtig ist, die Köpfe der
metallenen Nadeln vorher Grün
zu besprühen. Dazu die Nadeln
in ein Stück Styropor stecken und
mit Farbe besprühen.

A straw wreath serves as the
base, on which the *Ilex* leaves
are arranged in all directions
and secured with pins. The
important thing is to spray the
metal heads of the pins with
green paint beforehand. To do
this, stick them in a piece of
Styrofoam and spray the paint
on them.

SEITE 185

Leuchtender letzter Gruß
Kranzkörper: Strohrömer, *Pinus strobus*
Kranzschmuck: Getrocknete *Acer*-Blätter, Zweige von *Betula*, *Chysanthemum Cultivar*, *Hedera helix*, *Hypericum calycinum*, *Salix sachalinensis*, *Thuja occidentalis*, *Typha latifolia*

PAGE 185

Luminous farewell
wreath base: straw wreath, *Pinus strobus*
wreath embellishment: dried *Acer* leaves, *Betula* twigs, *Chysanthemum cultivar*, *Hedera helix*, *Hypericum calycinum*, *Salix sachalinensis*, *Thuja occidentalis*, *Typha latifolia*

SEITE 186

Kranz mit Blattspiel
Kranzkörper: Weidenkranz
Kranzschmuck: *Erica herbacea*, *Euonymus fortunei*, *Gaultheria procumbens*, *Hedera helix*, Ahornlaub, trockenes Gras

PAGE 186

Wreath with playful leaves
wreath base: wicker ring
wreath embellishment: *Erica herbacea*, *Euonymus fortunei*, *Gaultheria procumbens*, *Hedera helix*, maple leaves, dried grass

SEITE 187

Blättervielfalt
Kranzkörper: Weidenkranz
Kranzschmuck: *Heuchera*, *Ajuga reptans*, *Fragaria vesca*, *Geranium macrorrhizum*, *Geranium Cultivar*

PAGE 187

Foliage diversity
wreath base: wicker ring
wreath embellishment: *Heuchera*, *Ajuga reptans*, *Fragaria vesca*, *Geranium macrorrhizum*, *Geranium cultivar*

SEITE 188

An das Leben
Kranzkörper: Strohrömer, *Thuja plicata*
Kranzschmuck: *Carlina acaulis*, *Chamelaucium uncinatum*, *Cortaderia selloana*, *Hypericum calycinum*, *Lycopodium annotinum*, *Rosa Cultivar*, Band

PAGE 188

A toast to life
wreath base: straw wreath, *Thuja plicata*
wreath embellishment: *Carlina acaulis*, *Chamelaucium uncinatum*, *Cortaderia selloana*, *Hypericum calycinum*, *Lycopodium annotinum*, *Rosa cultivar*, ribbon

SEITE 189

**Christrosen –
Blüten des Winters**
Kranzkörper: Strohrömer
Kranzschmuck: *Abies procera*, *Cocos lucifera*, *Helleborus niger*, *Prunus spinosa*, Band

PAGE 189

**Christmas roses –
blooms of winter**
wreath base: straw wreath
wreath embellishment: *Abies procera*, *Cocos lucifera*, *Helleborus niger*, *Prunus spinosa*, ribbon

SEITE 190

Silberglanz
Kranzkörper: Weidenkranz
Kranzschmuck: *Calocephalus brownii*, *Eucalyptus*-Fruchtzweige, *Santolina*, *Senecio bicolor*, getrocknete Maisblätter

PAGE 190

Silver sheen
wreath base: wicker ring
wreath embellishment: *Calocephalus brownii*, *Eucalyptus* fruit branches, *Santolina*, *Senecio bicolor*, dried corn leaves

SEITE 191

Kostbare Winterblüten
Kranzkörper: Weidenkranz
Kranzschmuck: *Euphorbia maritima*, *Helleborus niger*, Ligusterbeeren, *Stachys*-Fruchtstände

PAGE 191

Precious winter blooms
wreath base: wicker ring
wreath embellishment: *Euphorbia maritima*, *Helleborus niger*, privet berries, *Stachys* inflorescence

SEITE 192/193

Laminierte Lunaria
Kranzkörper: Mooswulst
Kranzschmuck: Papier, grün gestrichene Schaschlikspieße, *Lunaria annua*, *Rubus fruticosus*

PAGE 192/193

Laminated Lunaria
wreath base: moss ring
wreath embellishments: paper, kebab skewers picks painted green, *Lunaria annua*, *Rubus fruticosus*

Die noch grünen *Lunaria*-Fruchtstände auf Papier kleistern, laminieren, in Quadrate schneiden, auf grüne Schaschlikspieße stecken. Als Abschluss Brombeeren aufsetzen.

Glue green *Lunaria* seed pods to a sheet of paper, laminate, cut in squares and skewer on green-painted kebab sticks. Finish off the tips of the sticks with blackberries.

**GESTECKE
BASED TRIBUTES**

SEITE 210

Sommerlich mit Kosmee
Schleifenband, Unterlage, *Cosmos bipinnatus*, *Dianthus barbatus*, *Heuchera micrantha*, *Lavandula angustifolia*, *Limonium latifolium*, *Pelargonium Cultivar*, *Rosa Cultivar*, *Salvia officinalis*, *Spiraea japonica*, verschiedene Kräuter

PAGE 210

Summery tribute with cosmos
banner, base, *Cosmos bipinnatus*, *Dianthus barbatus*, *Heuchera micrantha*, *Lavandula angustifolia*, *Limonium latifolium*, *Pelargonium cultivar*, *Rosa cultivar*, *Salvia officinalis*, *Spiraea japonica*, assorted herbs

SEITE 211

Sommerlich in Blau-Violett
Band, Unterlage, Organzaband, *Ageratum houstonianum*, *Clematis vitalba*, *Eucalyptus cinerea*, *Hydrangea macrophylla*, *Lathyrus odoratus*, *Limonium latifolium*, *Nigella damascena*, *Salvia officinalis*, *Salvia viridis*, *Scabiosa caucasia*, *Senecio cineraria*

PAGE 211

**Summery tribute
in blue and purple**
ribbon, base, organza ribbon, *Ageratum houstonianum*, *Clematis vitalba*, *Eucalyptus cinerea*, *Hydrangea macrophylla*, *Lathyrus odoratus*, *Limonium latifolium*, *Nigella damascena*, *Salvia officinalis*, *Salvia viridis*, *Scabiosa caucasia*, *Senecio cineraria*

SEITE 211

Sommerlich in Rose-Violett
Band, Unterlage, *Achillea millefolium*, *Astrantia major*, *Cotinus coggygria*, *Dianthus plumarius*, *Lathyrus latifolius*, *Lathyrus odoratus*, *Nigella damascena*, *Origanum vulgare*, *Pseudolysimachion longifolium*, *Rosa Cultivar*

PAGE 211

**Summery tribute
in pink and purple**
ribbon, base, *Achillea millefolium*, *Astrantia major*, *Cotinus coggygria*, *Dianthus plumarius*, *Lathyrus latifolius*, *Lathyrus odoratus*, *Nigella damascena*, *Origanum vulgare*, *Pseudolysimachion longifolium*, *Rosa cultivar*

SEITE 212

Bukett mit Tulpen und Rosen
Unterlage aus Holz mit Steckschaum und Moos, Band, *Chamelaucium uncinatum*, *Helleborus foetidus*, *Rosa Cultivar*, *Tulipa Cultivar*, diverse Trockengräser und Zweige

PAGE 212

Bouquet with tulips and roses
wooden base with floral foam and moss, banner, *Chamelaucium uncinatum*, *Helleborus foetidus*, *Rosa cultivar*, *Tulipa cultivar*, assorted dried grasses and twigs

SEITE 212

Bukett mit Rosen und Amaryllis
Unterlage aus Holz mit Steckschaum und Moos, Band, *Cordyline Cultivar*, *Cytisus x hollandica*, *Gerbera jamesonii*, *Hippeastrum Cultivar*, *Hyacinthus orientalis*, *Rosa Cultivar*, *Ranunculus asiaticus*, diverses Beiwerk

PAGE 212

Bouquet with roses and amaryllis
wooden base with floral foam and moss, ribbon, *Cordyline cultivar*, *Cytisus x hollandica*, *Gerbera jamesonii*, *Hippeastrum cultivar*, *Hyacinthus orientalis*, *Rosa cultivar*, *Ranunculus asiaticus*, assorted embellishments

SEITE 213

Bukett mit Gerbera und Nelken
Unterlage aus Holz mit Steckschaum und Moos, Band, *Chamelaucium uncinatum*, *Dianthus caryophyllus*, *Gerbera jamesonii*

PAGE 213

**Bouquet with
gerberas and carnations**
wooden base with floral foam and moss, ribbon, *Chamelaucium uncinatum*, *Dianthus caryophyllus*, *Gerbera jamesonii*

SEITE 214

Blütenkissen mit Bleikreuz
Unterlage, Band, Bleiband, *Dahlia*, *Gypsophila `Million Star`*, *Lysimachia clethroides*, *Sanvitalia procumbens*, *Sedum floriferum*, verschiedene gelbe und weiße Blüten

Der gewundene Kranz, der das
Gesteck umgibt, besteht aus
verschiedenen Werkstoffen. Die
Stielenden werden zur Wasserversorgung in den Steckschaum
gesteckt, dann außen herum um
die Mitte geführt und wieder an
der Steckbasis befestigt.

The interwoven wreath encircling
the assembly is made of a variety
of materials. The stem ends are
inserted in the floral foam to keep
them supplied with water, then
looped around the posy and again
secured to the base.

In eine dreieckige Konstruktion git-
terförmig zueinander angebrachter
Aststücke wird die Steckunterlage
eingebaut und mit *Muehlenbeckia*-
Gerank kaschiert. Das lässt die
strenge Form weicher erscheinen.

The foam base is integrated in the
three-cornered construction of
branches and then covered with
Muehlenbeckia vines. This softens
the strict outline somewhat.

Alle im Buch abgebildeten Blumen und Pflanzen sind im gut sortierten Blumengroßhandel erhältlich. Die verwendeten Kranz- oder Gesteckunterlagen sind über den Floristikbedarfsgroßhandel zu beziehen, ebenso alle technischen Hilfsmittel, sowie die abgebildeten Accessoires, Trauerkarten und anderen Materialien. Die abgebildeten Urnen und Särge sind Leihgaben deutscher Hersteller. Informationen hierzu über den entsprechenden Fachhandel.

Wir danken der Firma Halbach, Remscheid, für die Unterstützung bei der Realisation dieses Buches. Fast alle abgebildeten Bänder, Kordel, Litzen, Kranzschleifen stammen aus dem Hause Halbach:

All of the flowers and plants illustrated in this book are available at any well-stocked flower wholesaler's. The wreath and based tribute forms can be obtained from florist supply wholesalers, as can all technical aids and mechanics, as well as the accessories, sympathy cards and other materials used in the book. The illustrated urns and caskets were kindly loaned to us by German manufacturers. Information about them can be obtained in related retail outlets.

We would like to thank the Halbach company in Remscheid for their support in the production of this book. Almost all of the ribbons, cords, braids and wreath banners in the photographs were manufactured by Halbach:

Halbach-Seidenbänder Dekoband Vertrieb GmbH
Ritterstr. 15, 42899 Remscheid-Lüttringhausen, Germany
Tel. +49(0)2191-9583-0, Fax +49(0)2191-958399
www.halbach-seidenbaender.com

Mit Unterstützung von / Sponsored by